THE
CHRISTIAN
COUPLE

LARRY & NORDIS CHRISTENSON

THE CHRISTIAN COUPLE

BETHANY HOUSE PUBLISHERS

MINNEAPOLIS, MINNESOTA 55438

A Division of Bethany Fellowship, Inc.

The Scripture quotations in this publication, except where otherwise noted, are from the Revised Standard Version of the Bible, copyrighted 1946 and 1952 by the Division of Christian Education of the National Council of Churches of Christ in the U.S.A. and used by permission.

Published by Bethany Fellowship, Inc.
6820 Auto Club Road, Minneapolis, Minnesota 55438

Printed in the United States of America

Library of Congress Cataloging in Publication Data

Christenson, Laurence.
    The Christian couple.

    Bibliography: p.
    1. Marriage. I. Christenson, Nordis, joint author.
II. Title.
BV835.C47   248'.4   77-24085
ISBN 0-87123-051-8

This book is lovingly dedicated to two Christian
couples who celebrated their golden wedding
anniversaries while we were writing it—
our parents—
Ade and Mimi Christenson,
Tim and Ann Evenson

Acknowledgment

Many of the examples used in this book come out of our personal experience and correspondence. In most cases, however, the names have been changed and the settings and incidents sufficiently altered to protect the privacy of individuals.

Preface

An actor, well known for his romantic roles, was asked on a TV talk-show, "What makes a 'great lover'?"

He answered, "A great lover is someone who can satisfy one woman all her life long; and who can be satisfied by one woman all his life long. A great lover is not someone who goes from woman to woman to woman. Any dog can do that."

To satisfy a woman is the hallmark of a lover, and a deep affirmation of one's manhood. It finds expression not only in the sexual relationship but in every aspect of the marriage. When a man gets a promotion, or opens the door for his wife, or fixes something around the house, or takes charge of an unruly brood of children, he wants to know that he has satisfied his wife. Not just that he has pleased her, but satisfied her, which means that she identifies herself with him in what he has done. To satisfy a woman is one of the deepest expressions of real manhood.

We are writing this book because we have come to the conviction that we live in a time when men need to be challenged to succeed *as men*. This means more than succeeding in their careers. It means succeeding in that which is basic to all human life and society—marriage and the home.

You *can* succeed as a husband and as a man.

That is the simple theme of this book. Indeed, succeeding as a husband is a large part of what it means to succeed as a man.

FOR WIVES

The air is shrill today with the cry for "rights," stirring up envy and resentment for real or imagined wrongs done against women. In the midst of this we need to hear the voice of God. We need the guidance and assurance of His wisdom.

Is your heart at rest in the attitudes and priorities which you have chosen, or which have been pressed upon you?

Our calling as wives centers in our relationship with those closest to us, our husband and children. We know within ourselves that serving and relating to them is our first obligation. Under God it can also be our greatest joy, for it harmonizes with our God-given calling to be "a helper fit for him."

> A man who takes a wife has a helper fit for him, and a pillar to lean upon. If kindness and gentleness are on her tongue, her husband has no equal among the sons of men.—Sirach 36:23

Are we as wives satisfied with our family life? Are we ready to forgive where there has been hurt? Are we confident that we have the right direction, and are we growing in accomplishment?

We are writing this book because we believe that women want to grow in relating effectively to their husbands. That is where true happiness lies for us as wives. God's wisdom and grace can bring a new quality of happiness to our marriages. And having a happy marriage is a large part of what it means to be a happy woman.

Contents

PART ONE

Pioneers

For this reason a man shall leave his father and mother and be joined to his wife, and the two shall become one.
—Ephesians 5:31

CHAPTER ONE

The Challenge

Marriage is like the conquest and settling of a new land. When you cross from single to married life it is like a pioneer crossing the Mississippi River in 1840 —a new unexplored territory stretches out before you. No matter how many people may have settled down in marriage before, it is still a new and unsettled land for each couple that enters into it.

Pioneering links together two things which often strive against each other in marriage. The first thing is *hope*. Pioneers enter a new territory with great hopes. They envision the home and wealth and future which will be theirs in this new land.

The second thing pioneers experience is *difficulty*. This new land does not yield up its treasure without a struggle. Pioneers run up against obstacles and forces which would drive them back and keep them from settling the land.

All too often in marriage hope shrivels up in the face of difficulty. Difficulty, when it comes, is greeted with dismay, and gives way to discouragement. A sharp disagreement between husband and wife, a problem in sexual adjustment, a difference over finances—virtually any real difficulty—can cut the nerve of hope.

Our age has mis-taught us concerning marriage. We have been led to believe that marriage is all hope and no difficulty. Our heads have been crammed with happily-ever-after fairy tales and with Hollywood romances. Marriage is the land of hopes and dreams, where a couple encounters no difficulties as long as they are "right for each other."

The true pioneer does not greet difficulty as something strange. He does not quail before it. It does not quench his hope but rather heightens it. From the beginning these two things were linked together in his mind, the hope and the difficulty. He believes in the hope, but he has not deluded himself that it would fall easily into his hand. There is a price to pay, a price of struggle, endurance, and, yes, of faith. Against all difficulty one must believe in the hope of this new land. And therefore the pioneer does not retreat from difficulty, nor does he ignore it. He meets it and deals with it because of the hope.

Step by step he settles the land. He wins from it the riches that are stored up there for him and his family. He is practical and resourceful. He fashions solutions out of things at hand. He develops the capacity to adjust to unexpected situations. He is willing to endure hardship. He sees problems as a normal part of pioneer life. He accepts difficulty as the price one must pay to tap the riches of the new land.

Such a venture is marriage, a pioneering venture. "A man leaves father and mother and is joined to his wife." With his wife he journeys into a new land. Hope and difficulty are their everyday companions, the raw material out of which they build the happiness and achievement of their life together. They are not content to loiter at the borderlands. They have set their faces to the West, and they mean to explore this new land to the fullest.

This is the challenge of marriage. This is the challenge to one who calls himself a husband, the challenge to lead his wife into the pioneering of a new land.

Marriage Is the 'New Land' Pioneer Land
FULL OF DIFFICULTY FULL OF HOPE

CHAPTER TWO

The Crisis

There is a sobering side to pioneer history: Some did not make it. The difficulties proved too formidable and rose up and overwhelmed them.

Every generation has seen some of its marriages fall by the wayside. Yet people continue to pour into marriage, marking the casualties with a kind of grim forbearance as a toll that society pays for the extension of family life. But today the difficulties facing marriage appear to have reached crisis proportions. Some social scientists are convinced that the death of the family is at hand. Ferdinand Lundberg, author of *The Coming World Transformation*, says that the family "is near the point of complete extinction." [1]

Millions of young adults appear to be disillusioned with conventional marriage and are experimenting with life-styles different from those of their parents. Values that have helped shape Western civilization for centuries are being called into question—lifelong commitment, parental responsibility, and distinct roles for man and wife.[2] Marriage, this 'new land' that has swept generation after generation to its bosom, for some seems to be losing its lure. There is a rebellion against the rigor of its climate and its totalitarian claim upon one's life.

On every side the venture of marriage is plagued with uncertainty. People who are already married see happiness and fulfillment eroded away with each passing year, and wonder whether they are clinging to the empty shell of a dream. Young people enter into marriage with a distinct inner reserve; they may not call it a "trial marriage," but practically speaking that is the extent of the underlying commitment which our age has shaped in them. Even those who are happily married experience pangs of dismay and helplessness as the marriages of close friends and relatives break up before their eyes.

Both the number and the rate of divorces continue to mount. In 1960 there were 25 divorces for every 100 marriages; in 1975, 48 per 100; in 1990, at the present rate of increase, there will be 63 divorces for every 100 marriages—a 150 percent increase in one generation.[3]

Divorce is only the tip of the iceberg. How much frustration, discontent, and wretchedness hulks under the surface in marriages that have not come to divorce? A popular newspaper columnist conducted a survey and found that 77 percent of the married women interviewed said they would rather not be married.

Yet the paradox is this: Despite the gloom, an overwhelming majority still see marriage as the place they want to be, the 'new land' of hopes and dreams. A survey by the Institute of Life Insurance found that 87 percent of the respondents over 29 years of age chose a "happy family life" as the most important goal of their lives—a distant second was "developing as an individual," with 7 percent.[4]

But how to attain it, amidst the crises of our times? How can a couple carve out a successful and happy life in this territory called marriage, when more and more people are turning back or falling by the wayside?

Analyzing the Crisis

The widespread crisis in family life presents husband, wife, and children—indeed, society at large—with a clutch of problems, but also with opportunities. Crisis is not necessarily bad. It can bring us to a point of decision where we choose a better way than the one we have been following. If right decisions are made we may see better marriages emerging from the crisis—healthier, freer, more creative and loving than even idealized stereotypes out of the past.

What is the reason for the crisis in family life? Is it brought about by the cross-currents of turmoil which characterize our times—disorder, fragmentation, youth rebellion, sexual revolution, political disillusion, women's liberation? Is social upheaval subjecting the family to more stress than it can handle? Have we entered an age where the family must either undergo structural change, or else be set aside?

History might give us some answers. Perhaps the family has faced crises like this in times past, and if so, could we profit from that experience?

Historical studies on the family, however, have come into vogue only recently. Prior to the publication of Philippe Aries' study of family life in 1960,[5] historians' references to the family were generally limited to its legal and institutional aspects, with occasional allusions to changes in the manners and mores of society.[6] Careful historical research on the family—and specifically on how the family has faced up to social change—is meager.

Anthropologists and sociologists provide us with some understanding of the structure of family life in other cultures. Biography can be a rich source of information and insight into family life, but by its very nature biography focuses on a small segment of society and covers a relatively short span of time. Our historical understanding of the family is pieced together from scattered references and impressions, and for that reason it is particularly susceptible to generalized stereotypes.

"We need to get back to the kind of family life our grandparents and great-grandparents had!" You hear it said confidently, as though one were stating a self-evident truth.

The cynic snorts and declares with equal confidence that family life back then was no better than it is now. In fact, behind the facade, it was probably worse.

The fact of the matter is, we don't know. Parents, grandparents, and great-grandparents may give us some idea of the way things were. But how typical would one family be of a whole culture? And how much that is vital to family life gets skipped over in the normal sharing that goes on between one generation and another? How many people, for instance, have more than a smattering of knowledge about the sexual relationship of their grandparents, or the impact this may have had on the life of the family? How many children could describe accurately the way their own parents learned to work out differences? What does the average person know about the internal family dynamics even of close relatives and friends?

Comprehensive and reliable data on family life in past cultures—or even in our own—is hard to come by. A degree of secrecy is inherent in the very structure of family life. Our contacts with other people are mostly outside the family setting. It is extremely difficult for an outsider to break through the barrier of exclusiveness and see another family as it really is. Much more so to penetrate the family walls of past generations.

Family life has undoubtedly faced crises in other times and other cultures. But the record of it is available to us only in limited degree, as though to tell us, "You must look beyond here for help."

The lack of detailed information from the past can actually be an advantage in facing the present crisis in family life. Since we cannot spell out in detail the family practices of past generations, we are forced to give up the illusion that we can solve today's problems by a simplistic return to the way things used to be. It is tempting to retreat into the past when one's security seems threatened. But a retreat into the past can become a substitute for realistic involvement in the present.

This does not mean that the past has nothing to offer us. No realistic answer to the crisis in family life can turn its back on the past. But we must understand clearly what it is that the past offers us. It is not a detailed report on family life which we can simply transplant into our own time. It is rather an *understanding* of family life in terms of certain basic principles. Past generations have not left us an exhaustive description of family life, but they have left us considerable teaching on the nature, structure, and purpose of the family.[7] It is this understanding of family life which we must weigh.

It is one of the conceits of our time that we hold the thinking of the past in widespread contempt. It thus made news when eighteen top theologians drafted a document challenging many of the basic assumptions of modern Christian theology. The first and pivotal section of the "Hartford Affirmation" rejects the idea that "modern thought is superior to all past forms of understanding reality, and is therefore normative for Christian faith and life." [8]

Wisdom is not the product of mere abstract thinking. It has a historical root structure; it grows out of experience. Those who scorn the cumulation of wisdom from the past deprive themselves of truth which has been won at the cost of struggle and suffering. The past can speak to us about mistakes to be avoided; solutions which have proven effective.

Is modern thought on marriage and the family the last word in wisdom? Has it produced the kind of results we want to see multiplied? If a particular medicine were prescribed for a malady, and the net result were that the sickness would spread more widely, would we not call the prescription into question? Is it not possible that the present crisis in marriage and family life comes from having taken the wrong prescription, and that to continue the same prescription will only lead to a further spreading of the sickness? What is needed is a different prescription.

A Different Prescription

In addressing ourselves to the present crisis in marriage and family life, we would raise a basic challenge: the challenge to consider intelligently a prescription for marriage which is rooted not in the thought structure of modern culture but in the thought structure of the Bible.

Biblical principles of family life are sometimes greeted—and rejected—with a rhetorical show of horror: "You can't be serious! After all, we're living in the 20th century!" As though we could learn nothing from the past; as though the beliefs and values of our culture were beyond questioning. Has the 20th century produced the kind of marriage and family life that warrants such blind faith in its prescriptions?

The danger in our time is not that we will lapse into outmoded social patterns from the past. As we have seen, the past does not make available to us detailed patterns of family life; what we have from the past are principles which offer a possible basis for building family life. Our danger is that we will be intimidated by the *Zeitgeist* ("the spirit of the times"), and never give a reasonable hearing to any ideas which run contrary to the spirit of our own age.

One of the very reasons for the crisis in family life is that we have too uncritically given way to the slogans of contemporary thought. Biblical ideas on family life are rejected simply because they are out of phase with the spirit of the times.

We will not solve the crisis in family life by clamping on 20th-century blinders, and smugly dismissing anything outside the furrows of contemporary thought. We need a broader vision.

This is especially true for Christians living in the second half of the 20th century. Over the past 300 years the organism of Western civilization has been nourished less and less at the bosom of the Christian faith, but more and more at the cribs of secular humanism. In our own century the outcome of this shift has become evident: Our culture cannot stomach the vital core of the Christian faith. Christianity and secular humanism are fundamentally at variance with one another.[9]

Those who are Christians, living in this society, must therefore examine with the greatest care the beliefs and assumptions which underlie contemporary diagnoses for the ills that afflict marriage. For if we accept a prescription for marriage completely dependent upon the belief-structure of secular humanism, then we must be prepared that the result will be something other than *Christian* family life.

The Bible offers a significant thought structure on marriage and family life. It merits intelligent consideration.

On the one hand, therefore, we are saying, "Do not scorn biblical principles simply because they come from another era. Consider what the Bible says about marriage, and whether it does not speak meaningfully to our generation as it has to hundreds before ours; indeed, whether it does not speak personally to you."

On the other hand, however, we are saying that taking biblical principles seriously does not mean a simplistic "return to the past." Principles that are true have an enduring validity, but the way in which they are applied will vary from one age to another.

What is needed is an appreciation of the fundamental validity of what the Bible says about marriage, then a sensitivity to the Holy Spirit as one seeks to apply it in everyday life. Both elements are necessary. If we brush aside what the Bible says about marriage, we deprive ourselves of a base from which to challenge many of the assumptions of our culture which, if they go unchallenged, will continue to produce the kind of family life that has brought on the present crisis. On the other hand, biblical truth cannot be rigidly applied as so many abstract principles. At its core, biblical truth is a *Person.* Biblical truth is applied to a marriage when the *living Christ* schools and leads husband and wife in their daily life. The Bible gives us a clear idea of what we may expect, the general approach to marriage which Jesus takes. But only the Holy Spirit can relate us to Christ in such a way that His presence and His plan becomes a lived-out reality in our marriage.

PRESCRIPTION FOR MARRIAGE

Biblical Principles Put Into Practice Under the Leading of the Holy Spirit

CHAPTER THREE

The Call

*Dearly beloved, we are gathered together here in
the sight of God, and in the face of this company,
to join together this man and this woman in holy
matrimony; which is an honourable estate, instituted
by God.* —The Book of Common Prayer

I don't remember exactly when it came upon me.
It was probably gradual. And it was sometime after
we had been married about ten years. It dawned
on me as a thought, and then became a conviction,
which, more than any other single thing, has liber-
ated my understanding of what marriage really is.

Marriage is something which has been instituted
by God. It belongs to Him. He does not hand it over
to man to do with as he pleases. He calls people into
it. It brings, or can bring, blessing to the man and
woman entering it, but that is corollary to its main
purpose, which is to fulfill the intention of God.
"Those who enter marriage," Dietrich Bonhoeffer
said, "enter upon a station, a commission, a trust."

Marriage belongs to God. That is a liberating
truth.

It sets us free, first of all, from the untruth that
marriage belongs to us. If marriage belongs to us,
then we can use it, abuse it, set it aside, suspend
it, or restructure it however it suits us. A marriage
that belongs to us will suffer at the hands of selfish-

ness and immaturity, even sheer impulse and whim.

Secondly, it sets us free from the untruth that we belong to marriage. If we belong to marriage, then our participation can too easily deteriorate to the level of mere obligation. To be locked into marriage, as an impersonal institution, may offer a degree of stability. But it also means that stifling misery can be inflicted on us by a mate, or by other family members, even by the standards and restraints of society as a whole.

It is a different matter when we see that marriage is a *trust*. A trust implies another party who has an interest, indeed the primary interest, in that which is put into trust. God has a high stake in marriage: He entrusts the foundation and therefore the future of human society to those who enter marriage. Furthermore, He *supports* them in the marriage, and that is all-important. Divine resources are available to marriage "under God."

A trust involves accountability. I must give account of that which has been entrusted to me—give account to *him who appointed me to the trust.*

It is sobering, and yet at the same time liberating, to realize that I am accountable to *God* for my marriage. Sobering because I know that His expectations are high, and there is no hiding anything from Him. Yet liberating because it is easier to answer to one master than to many.

Before this truth took root in my life our marriage was beset with a clamor of bosses, each one presenting his own particular opinion or demand: myself, my wife, the children, friends and relatives, "authorities on marriage," church leaders, society at large. Each one, on any given occasion, may have something valuable to offer. But my final accountability for the marriage is not to any of them, myself and my wife included, but to God.

Of course this truth, like any truth, could be abused. A man could use the "will of God" to camouflage his own selfish interests. But where a man honestly seeks to answer to God for what happens in the marriage, this truth can bring an extraordinary experience of freedom. By this we do not mean the short-lived freedom that is pandered to the ego, the freedom to do what you want to do; but the freedom that is a steadfast call to the spirit, the freedom to *become* what God has given you the potential to become. "Where the Spirit of the *Lord* is, there is *freedom*" (2 Cor. 3:17).

God sees our potential in grand design, but we do not. For us it comes quietly into being through the thousand little decisions of everyday life in which we seek His will for the marriage which He has entrusted to us.

* * *

Ken Whyte, a successful young executive, came home one evening feeling that he had turned an important corner. But he wasn't sure just how his wife would take it. He eased the car into the garage until the front bumper touched the suitcase which he had left there two days ago for his wife to take down to the luggage shop, so it could be repaired in time for their vacation.

"That's one errand she can forget about," he thought to himself, recalling his experience in the office that afternoon. He had been stopped short in the middle of preparing a report with the distinct impression that he should pray about their vacation plans. It was so unmistakable that he did it right on the spot. The certainty which came was just as distinct: He knew they must change their plans. It wasn't the way he had wanted it personally, yet once he accepted it, it brought a quiet sense of resolution.

A self-conscious smile traced briefly across his lips, as he thought about telling his wife that he had come around to her way of thinking. He wondered how she would react to the prayer thing.

"What's for dinner?" he asked, passing by the kitchen.

"I don't know, Mr. Bigshot. Rummage around for yourself. I've already eaten." His wife's voice came from the living room alcove, where she was writing at the antique desk they had inherited from an eccentric old matriarch on his wife's side of the family.

"What's the deal?" he asked matter-of-factly, coming to the archway between the living room and the outside entrance.

"No deal. I just had late coffee with Jan, and have some letters to write. I'm not hungry."

"Well, I *didn't* have late coffee, and I *am* hungry." He spoke firmly, but without petulance.

"Mr. Bigshot's hungry."

"What's this 'Mr. Bigshot' all of a sudden?"

"Isn't that you—Mr. Bigshot? Rising young executive. The fairhaired boy. Vice-president in another five or six years if you watch your P's and Q's. Weekends and evenings. Sometimes 6:30, sometimes 7:30, sometimes 9:00 or 10:00."

"What are you complaining about tonight? I'm home on time."

"Send off a rocket."

"Boy, are you in a foul mood."

"I'm in a very good mood. I had a long talk with

Jan this afternoon, and I realized that my whole life doesn't have to revolve around Mr. Bigshot. I've been putting off writing these letters for three weeks. So I decided you could fix supper for yourself."

He compressed his lips, the way he always did when he was weighing a decision. He glanced at the front door which, oddly, stood a few inches ajar. He walked over and put his hand to the door knob, turning it back and forth several times. Then he closed it smartly, and turned the latch. He walked back to the kitchen, opened the refrigerator, and began to assemble the makings of a light supper.

He was halfway through a cold cheese sandwich, gazing idly at the wall-hanging beside the telephone, embroidered with some religious saying in Italian, when his wife came in from the living room. He didn't notice her until he heard the refrigerator door click open.

"Want a glass of milk with your sandwich?" she asked quietly.

"Okay."

His matter-of-fact tone didn't surprise her. In twelve years of marriage she had learned that he had a way of dismissing unpleasant situations from his mind.

At times she found it maddening, because things that bothered her never seemed to get resolved. But she had no capacity for enduring prolonged estrangement. She was like her fiery Sicilian mother, who, scolding any one of her nine children to speechless shame, would invariably strike on some excuse within the next quarter hour to embrace that child and speak some word of endearment.

He watched her as she poured out a glass of milk and brought it to the table.

"Thanks." He spoke the word simply and naturally. Sarcasm was something which had been bred out of his nature by a long line of New England Puritans, who lived by the dictum, "Say what you mean, and mean what you say." In some ways it made him an easy person to live with. While he could be devastatingly frank, he was almost never devious, and he stored up little rancor.

"The man at the luggage shop said he can't fix the suitcase," she said.

"I was wondering about that when I drove in. I didn't know you had taken it down."

"He has to send away for a whole new lock. It'll take three weeks and cost about twelve dollars."

He nodded, without speaking.

"It won't be ready for the vacation." She said it without inuendo, but couldn't bring herself to say "our" vacation. For the past month they had been arguing about this vacation. Two other couples from the company had invited them to go along on a vacation to Washington and New York. They weren't even close friends, and were the kind of party-party people she didn't like anyway. It was her idea of no vacation. But he said it would be good for his job, so they had arranged for someone to stay with the kids while they took off for what she envisioned as a two-week endurance test of restaurants, theaters, art galleries, museums, and night clubs.

"I've done some thinking about 'the vacation,' " he said.

She looked at him quizzically. It wasn't like him to mimic her.

"As a matter of fact, I prayed about it this afternoon."

"You did?" She registered interest, but not real

surprise, which made it easier for him to continue.

"I did," he continued, nodding his head slowly. "And I think we ought to change our plans. If we wait till summer, we can go somewhere with the kids—to a lake, or camping."

"And not go to Washington and New York?" she asked incredulously. "What will they say?"

"I don't know," he said, shrugging his shoulders.

"What'll you tell them?"

"Just tell them we've changed our minds."

They didn't speak for a few moments, and then she said, "Honey, you don't know how happy that would make me."

He smiled, and slid over to the telephone. He looked up the number of the man who had invited them on the vacation, and called him to say that they wouldn't be going.

"My wife and I have talked it over," he explained, "and we've decided to wait until summer to take our vacation. The kids want to go fishing, so maybe we'll camp, or take a cabin at one of the lakes . . ."

So simple and easy. He was a real diplomat. She didn't really hear the rest of the conversation. The way he started it out—those words hovered about her like a warm presence. *"My wife and I have talked it over . . ."*

When he had hung up, she kept looking at him. Slowly she reached across the table and laid her hand upon his. Without looking at her, he took her hand between his, lifted it, and kissed each of her fingers.

That talk with Jan seemed like it was a million miles away.

* * *

It is not typical in 20th-century Western culture for a man to test his family decisions with prayer. Nor does one, by natural inclination, give up his own way; especially when that way has been hammered out in the heat of controversy. Yet this is the kind of challenge which a Christian husband must face day by day. He cannot be content with the settled ways of secular society. Those ways have brought the family to stagnation, despair, and breakup. Marriage under God challenges a man to leave those ways behind in order to pioneer a new way of life.

How does a husband become a pioneer? He apprentices himself to *the* Pioneer. He becomes a committed disciple of Jesus Christ, who is called "the pioneer of our faith" (Heb. 12:2). A man's success as a husband hinges upon this relationship. "The head of every man is Christ, the head of a woman is her husband" (I Cor. 11:3). A man who expects to be a leader in his home must first of all become a follower of Jesus Christ.

A pioneer leads primarily by example. He discovers the way to go, then others are drawn after him. He does the thing that needs to be done, then others gain confidence to do it also. He does not demand, he demonstrates.

As a pioneer, a husband opens the way for himself and his wife to discover the unexplored vistas of marriage—the soaring mountain ranges of sexual fulfillment, the broad meadows of daily work, the untapped wealth of shared experience, the quiet lakes of reflection and repose, the shaded groves where new life comes to birth, the valleys of sorrow, discouragement, and defeat, the desert stretches where life and love struggle for bare existence, the swift rivers that challenge access to new opportunities. The horizon of marriage is new each morning, beckoning to further exploration of a dominion whose landscape is always changing, whose treasure is inexhaustible, whose promise is a call to unremitting hope.

MARRIAGE BELONGS TO GOD

PART TWO

Lovers

Husbands should love their wives as their own bodies. "For this reason a man shall leave his father and mother and be joined to his wife, and the two shall become one."

—Ephesians 5:28, 31

CHAPTER FOUR

How Should I Love My Wife?

You take care of something you love. That only makes sense. If you take good care of your car, it's going to run better. Take good care of your business and it will return a better profit. Take good care of your body and you'll stay in better health. Take good care of your wife and she'll be a better helpmate.

That sounds like a terribly selfish kind of love. It might be all right with a car or a business, even with your own body. But where another person is involved, why, that's exploitation! We might heap loads of neglect on a wife, but let it never be said that we exploit her!

We have trouble with this kind of a concept of love because we do not appreciate how radical the biblical understanding of marriage really is. We think of it as simply a relationship between two people. The Bible sees husband and wife as a unity. "They are no longer two but one" (Matt. 19:6).

A pretentious man might set up a standard like this: "I will love my wife for her own sake, asking nothing in return." How selfless! How spiritual! I can tell you that a man like that would be insufferable to live with. Patronizing. Cold. Distant. To say nothing of the fact that he would never come close to living up to his pious pretensions.

The Bible is at once more profound and more

practical. It sees a husband's love for his wife spring-
ing not from disinterested altruism, but from a profound personal unity. "Husbands should love their
wives as their own bodies. He who loves his wife
loves himself" (Eph. 5:28).

A man does not love his body out of lofty altruism. He loves it out of practical necessity. He needs
his body. He depends on it in everything he does.
If he expects his body to serve him well, he must
take care of it. He cannot take care of himself without
at the same time taking care of his body, for he
and his body are one.

So with his wife. He is one with her. His love
for her is an expression of his love for himself. It
does not spring from disinterested altruism, for that
would mean that they were two, not one. It springs
from their unity, and thus from honest self-interest.
Nor does the Bible frown on that. Jesus recognized
love of self as a reliable paradigm: "Love your neighbor *as yourself*" (Matt. 22:39).

Self-love is not self-centered indulgence. Wholesome love of self is outgoing and related to one's
calling in life. Why am I here? What is the purpose
of my life? I take care of myself in order that I
can do a better job at what I am called to do.

A busy executive told me that he had his secretary write in on his appointment schedule regular
conferences with "F.S.A. Hogh"—his private
acronym for a conference with "Father, Son, and
Holy Ghost." He had learned that when he allotted
regular time during the day to quiet focusing on God
he functioned more effectively both at the office and
at home. He told his secretary that his conferences
with F.S.A. Hogh were on a level with top corporate
policy meetings, to be interrupted only in exceptional
circumstances.

Recognizing the pressures that can build up in the world of corporate management, this man made a sensible decision to take care of himself. It helped him to fulfill his purpose more effectively—his purpose as an executive, as a husband, and as a man.

Another man I know regularly excused himself for bed at eight-thirty in the evening. He had lost one lung in a bout with tuberculosis, and he knew that he had to have extra rest if he were to continue to live and support his family. He took care of himself in order that he could take care of his responsibilities.

A man takes care of his wife like he takes care of himself, so she can fulfill and be fulfilled in her calling. That is the practical kind of love that grows out of a marriage where husband and wife are one.

The Bible says that God's intention in creating woman was to provide "a fitting helper" for man (Gen. 2:18). It is not a role imposed by culture or society. It is a God-ordained calling which harmonizes with God's purpose for her.

A husband who loves his wife will take care of her so she can fulfill this calling. It is a calling that will bless him; God meant it that way. But if he loves her as he loves himself, it is also a calling that will bring her personal fulfillment, for it accords with her God-created nature. Her husband wants fulfillment for her as he wants it for himself; he loves her as his own body.

I
AND
MY MATE
ARE
ONE

CHAPTER FIVE

Sensitive to Her Needs

How should I go about the business of loving my wife? What should I do, in practical terms?

Well, how, in practical terms, do we take care of our own bodies? That is the paradigm.

Two sensitivities guide us in taking care of our bodies. The first is this: We are sensitive to its *needs*. When my body needs food or clothing or a bath, I know about it. I have a built-in awareness.

What kind of needs does my wife have? I don't have a built-in awareness for it. It is a sensitivity I need to develop.

This and the next chapter present some of the things we have learned in the twenty-five years of our own marriage, as well as some seventeen years of marriage counseling, about a wife's needs.

She Needs To Be Affirmed

A wife needs to be affirmed *by her husband.* She needs to feel that she is important to him.

Affirmed as a Woman

She needs to know, first of all, that she is his *woman.* She needs to be affirmed sexually.

This means more than taking her to bed, though that is by no means unimportant. (We will be looking at the dynamics of the sexual relationship more explicitly in Chapter Seven.) But your wife's confidence in herself as a woman must extend beyond the bedroom. The quiet assurance that she is loved and cherished and wanted as a woman by a particular man must provide an undertone for her whole day.

That kind of assurance comes from the accumulation of many little affirmations. Jim Barker was a salesman who had gotten into the habit of starting to plan his day while he shaved. By the time he got his coat on and was heading out the door he was thoroughly immersed in his work, with scarcely a good-bye grunt for his wife. A friend who stopped by to pick him up twice a week noticed this and talked with him about it.

"It's a little hard for me to say this, Jim, but the way you leave your wife in the morning is downright impolite."

Jim saw the truth in it. He began stopping off in the kitchen for a good-bye kiss. One morning he was feeling a little expansive; he held his wife by the waist at arm's length and said, "You are something swell to come home to!"

"Well, I'll be waiting," she said with a knowing look.

"I think I may come home early," he said, picking up on her unanticipated banter.

Some time later Jim thanked the friend who had spoken to him. "I appreciate your being honest enough to have said that. It's made a real difference in our relationship. In fact, I can hardly believe that such a little thing could make such a big difference."

One man said, "I try at least once a day to remind my wife in some little way that she is sexually appealing to me." He was sixty-eight years old. His wife was a poised, accomplished woman, to whom many younger wives often turned for counsel.

A wife's sexuality, her self-confidence as a woman, will leave its mark on everything she does. It colors the way she keeps house, how she decorates her home, the way she stands beside her husband in public, the way she dons blue jeans and bandana to dig in the flower garden, the way she dresses the children, the way she works in the community, the way she listens to a friend over coffee, the way she compliments the check-out girl at the supermarket on a new hair-do.

There is something regal about a woman who comes beside her husband in public, takes his arm, and with never a word, but with her whole manner, makes the quiet assertion, "I am the woman of this man." There is a confidence and naturalness in relating to other people that marks a woman whose womanhood is deeply affirmed. The way a woman feels about her sexuality affects the way she relates to all of life.

Affirmed as a Wife

Secondly, a wife needs to know that her relationship with her husband is unique and God-ordained. She needs to be affirmed in her role as *wife*.

A young housewife we know told what a struggle she had over the business of being a "submissive" wife. She felt it would demean her. One day, after reading an article extolling the virtue of being a submissive wife, she said, "When my husband walked in the door that night, for all the world I wanted to raise the clenched fist of rebellion in his face!"

Yet she felt dissatisfied with the way things were going in their marriage. More-or-less as an experiment she decided to try the submissive thing. She began to listen more carefully to her husband, gave "sure" and "okay" wider berth in her vocabulary, tried to anticipate his preferences.

One evening, about a month later, they were scrunched together in the kitchen nook over a turkey sandwich while the kids were having TV suppers for a Walt Disney special. He put his arm around her and said, "Honey, I really enjoy coming home at night. Some of the group at the office work late or stop off for a drink on the way home. Seems they do anything they can to put off going home. I feel a peace the minute I come in the door. It's great."

She laughed telling us about it. "I still have to work at it, but let me tell you that for the week after that, 'submissive' was my joy word!"

Affirmed in her calling as a wife, she was able to see submissiveness in a new light. Not as something degrading, but as a good way of relating to someone who loves you and is responsible for you.*

Affirmation must be rooted in appreciation. The wife, above, initiated something that her husband genuinely appreciated. In voicing his appreciation he affirmed her. If you try to affirm your wife without truly appreciating her, it will come across as phony and patronizing.

The question to ask is not, "How can I affirm my wife?" Rather, "What do I appreciate about my wife—and how can I let her know it?"

---

*The biblical concepts of authority and submission differ from the general understanding that prevails in society, as Jesus indicated in Matthew 20:25-28. The application of these principles in the marriage relationship is discussed in Chapters Ten and Eleven.

Affirmed as a Person

Finally, and most important, because it undergirds everything else, a wife needs to feel that she is appreciated for herself; she is a unique individual, hand-crafted by the Creator, having special gifts and talents, and a style distinct from anyone else's. She needs to be affirmed as a *person*.

A woman once told me, "You should pay more attention to your wife. You ignore her in public."

A few weeks later we were travelling in the Midwest. Some couples in Ann Arbor, Michigan, asked us to meet with them and talk informally about family life. I made it my special intention to pay attention to Nordis all during the evening.

A good part of the evening was given to questions-and-answers. I looked right at Nordis and listened carefully every time she was answering a question. The more I looked at her and listened, the more I appreciated the wisdom and conviction with which she spoke.

How easily we come to take one another for granted! That woman had been right. I had allowed my appreciation for Nordis to become dulled. As I made a point simply of paying attention to her in this situation, I came to a fresh appreciation of her as a person.

A sense of appreciation doesn't develop automatically. It must be cultivated by conscious intention. And then it must be communicated in simple and natural ways—a word, a love-note, a compliment. Oftentimes the opportunity will arise spontaneously out of the situation.

At the end of the evening one of the young couples came up to chat with us. "It was so neat," the wife said, speaking to me, "how you kept looking at your wife and listening to what she said—like you were really one."

It felt good to be able to put my arm around Nordis and say, "Well, what she says is worth listening to!"

Silently I added, "Lord, don't let me forget it. Don't let me forget to appreciate that you have given me a wife who, along with everything else, has extra good common sense and judgment."

She Needs Status in Her Role as Homemaker

No person can function well if she is uncertain as to whether her status in life is valid or that what she does amounts to anything. It is not necessary that one's status be recognized widely by others. Status-seeking merely to inflate the ego can actually work to the detriment of personal growth. But in order to work effectively at any job, one must himself be convinced that what he is doing is worthwhile. And most of us need some encouragement in this, at least by those who are close to us and love us.

The role of homemaker is suffering a severe loss of status in our culture. A variety of social and economic factors have combined to move the home out of its historic position at the center of life. The family's provision of food and clothing, their education, health care, employment, entertainment, social life, and religious expression are centered to a large degree outside the home environment.

Considerable rhetoric in the feminist movement can be translated into the simple complaint, "Why can't we be where the important things are happening?" The home has become a sleeping and eating adjunct to the important activities of life. The center of life has moved, and the wife who still wants to be primarily a homemaker is made to feel it, painfully.

"You can't make your house and husband and kids your whole life. You have to get out into the world—find a job—become fulfilled!"

Many wives, who do not necessarily incline toward the feminist movement, nevertheless do suffer from the loss of status which has come to their traditional role as homemakers. They see their husbands wrapped up in their jobs, with little time for them, the children, or the home. They hear the society around them either downgrading the role of homemaker, or damning it with faint praise. They see their own children, as they grow up, finding fewer and fewer interests in the home. They see the media featuring women who are making a mark in the world; traditional homemakers seem almost by definition to be uninteresting, certainly not newsworthy. All around them they see people spending their major energies on activities which take place outside the home.

Generally speaking, a mother with small children has a full-time job right at home. When the children are a little older, she might turn some of her energies to meaningful work outside the home, work that would bring with it genuine status and fulfillment. But that cannot become a substitute for her status as a wife and homemaker, or it will further downgrade the importance of the family. Regardless of things outside the home that may command her attention, a wife needs to feel a particular and satisfying status as homemaker.

How does a husband do this? How does he give to his wife the status that she needs and deserves?

It is not just a matter of remembering to encourage and compliment her on the way she cooks and keeps house and raises the kids and mows the lawn and works on the PTA and washes and sews and irons and has a Brownie Troop and a dozen or so other activities, all the while keeping herself fresh and beautiful for her man. The compliments may do some good, but a more radical adjustment is called for.

I cannot give status to my wife's role as homemaker unless I give status to the home. And I can't do it with lip-service. No one is going to believe me, certainly not my wife, if I extol the importance of the home, but all the while my own interests and energies are centered somewhere else. The surest way to give status to my wife's role as homemaker is to let the home gain a heightened status in my own affections. If I want my wife to feel the importance of her role as homemaker, I must take seriously the importance of my role as head of the home.

Marriage remains an undiscovered reality, a far-off land, if the husband shows no interest in it. Much of the disorder and dissatisfaction in marriage today stems from the fact that husbands have given to marriage and the home a second- and third-rate priority. They have pursued the goals of job, career, and personal interests to the neglect of the home. Wife and children, following this lead, more and more turn their back on the home, seeking satisfaction and fulfillment elsewhere.

The feminist movement is a strident declaration that women cannot and will not homestead the domain of marriage and the family by themselves. If the husband assigns a low priority to the home, then the wife will downgrade it also. If job and business and career and competition and hobbies and status in the public marketplace, and any number of other activities, are more interesting to a husband than his marriage, then the wife will begin to look outside the marriage for her fulfillment also.

Feminists have tapped into a tragic reservoir of resentment on the part of women. But the real source of the resentment is not primarily that men have excluded women from full participation in the institutions and power structures of society. It is, rather, that men have withdrawn themselves from full and creative participation in the adventure of marriage. They have not given to marriage, and thus not given to their wives, the status and honor accorded by nature and by God. A woman resents this loss of status. Drawn by nature, and by all of human experience, to bind herself to a man in marriage, she feels cheated and betrayed when the marriage becomes a matter of secondary interest to her husband.

Men have relegated a too-low priority to the family. We charge it with the enormous responsibility of bringing up the next generation, and sustaining the present one, yet leave it more and more to shift for itself. Many of the ills of society trace back to lacks in the home, yet we continue to bumble along as though families will somehow run themselves.

They won't. Family life will continue to go downhill until husbands give it a higher personal priority. None of us will have a family worth the name unless we give it time and attention. What kind of 'success' is it if we make big splashes out in the world but fail at home?

How do I go about giving my home a higher priority? The key that opens the door is *time*. I must commit significant amounts of time to building up the life of my family.

I am not very handy at fixing things around the house, so my tendency is to put off the upkeep of the house and yard. My wife has had to put up with leaky faucets, dull knives, peeling paint, and poorly trimmed shrubs. A few years ago we struck on the idea of a two-hour work party every week. We were able to arrange everyone's schedule so that we could all put in a solid two-hour stint late Thursday afternoons. The boys and I worked on outside jobs, Nordis and the girls did a blitz of housecleaning. With a regular commitment of time we began to whittle down the backlog of undone jobs. And the upkeep of the house—often a burden that falls too heavily on the wife—became a family experience.

I saw a bumper sticker one day that said, "Happiness Is Weekly Family Night." We have tried to set aside Monday nights for the family. It has been only moderately successful. We often find it hard to come up with something to do that everyone will enjoy. We may read a book aloud, or sit around cracking walnuts, or play charades. We need more variety, more creativity. Our TV-culture tends to make us passive. Taking special time for the family is the first step. We are looking for ways to make the time count more effectively.

Of course the most important time we take for the family is the time we take for each other. Ralph and Ann Martin are members of a Christian community which has gone in for "extended households." In addition to their own children, they have six or seven other people living with them in their house. Every morning they leave the busy household and go to a nearby restaurant to have coffee together.

In the midst of a very busy life they spend an hour every day sipping coffee together. It is a wise investment of time. It accords the right kind of status to the responsibility they share of heading a household.

She Needs To Be Reminded That You Care

Love has a short memory. It needs continual reminders.

How long has it been since you wrote a love letter to your wife? I tried it once just for a lark and found out later that she had tucked it away in her little box labeled "Precious Memories." That told me something: What I had written was a) more important than I had thought, b) less frequent than I had ought.

In how many different ways this past week have you let on to your wife that you love and appreciate her? Love is inventive. It thinks up new ways of saying the same old wonderful thing.

One man stopped his children just as they were about to eat and said, "Everybody walk around the table and give Mommy a big love for this beautiful meal she fixed us!" So Mommy gathered in the loves of her three children, and a bear hug from her man (squeals from the bleachers), and the family sat down to a meal with appreciation accompanying the appetizer, and love the main course.

She Needs To Be Provided For

The needs we have been talking about have to do with a wife's feelings and attitudes, and they are in a sense primary: The way a woman feels about herself and her husband and her home will affect everything that happens in the home. If she feels appreciated and loved she has the most essential ingredient for her calling as a wife.

Of course a wife has other needs too. She needs to know that she will be provided for in terms of such things as—

Material necessities
Protection
Personal development
Sexual fulfillment
Spiritual growth

The husband's response to these kinds of needs will be taken up in some of the later chapters.

I & MY BODY ARE ONE

I & MY WIFE ARE ONE

MY BODY HAS NEEDS

MY WIFE HAS NEEDS

CHAPTER SIX

Sensitive to Her Hurts

The second sensitivity that guides us in taking care of our bodies is this: We are sensitive to its *hurts*. If I stub my toe or bang my head, I take special care of that part which is hurting.

The Bible tells husbands to be gentle, so as to cause their wives no hurt. "Love your wives, and do not be harsh with them" (Col. 3:19). The husband's spiritual leadership in the home depends upon the way he treats his wife. "Live considerately with your wives . . . that your prayers may not be hindered" (1 Pet. 3:7).

What kind of hurts does my wife have?

She May Be Hurting Physically

A husband needs to monitor carefully his wife's health and physical condition, just as he does his own. Someone has suggested that a husband's concern for his wife's health tends to degenerate over the years. This is suggested in "The Seven Ages of a Married Cold"—

First Year: "Sugar dumpling, I'm worried about my baby girl. You've got a bad sniffle. I'm putting you in the hospital for a general check-up and a good rest. I know the food's lousy, but I'll bring your meals in from Rossini's. I've already got it arranged."

Second Year: "Listen, darling, I don't like the

sound of that cough and I've called Doc Miller to rush over here. Now you go to bed like a good girl, please? Just for Papa."

Third Year: "Maybe you'd better lie down, honey; nothing like a little rest when you feel punk. I'll bring you something to eat. Where'd you put the soup?"

Fourth Year: "Look, dear, be sensible. After you feed the kids and get the dishes washed, you'd better hit the sack."

Fifth Year: "Why don't you get yourself a couple of aspirin?"

Sixth Year: "If you'd just gargle or something, instead of sitting around barking like a seal."

Seventh Year: "For Pete's sake, stop sneezing! What are you trying to do, give me pneumonia?"

Somewhere between these extremes—over-solicitousness and irritation—love will respond in a sensible way to a wife's sickness. But she can also be hurting physically short of sickness.

A wise woman, who had raised four children, once said to us, "A mother with small children has enough work to keep three people busy."

When you see that your wife is overtaxed physically, you need to sit down with her and make some sensible adjustments—

(1) Does she have the right priorities? She may be spreading herself too thin. If she is the kind that can't say 'no' to others, you may have to say it for her.

(2) Does she need some household help? If you can afford it, even a teenager coming in once a week to vacuum can be a real help.

(3) Is she doing some things that you ought to take over?

(4) Are the children being taught to help as soon as they're old enough?

(5) Are her standards of housekeeping, meal preparation, child care reasonable? A perfectionist needs to lower her standards. A sloppy housekeeper needs to take on her tasks one at a time and do a good job (even if some get left undone) so that she isn't churned up inside, dissipating her energies through a sense of fragmentation, frustration, and guilt.

(6) Does she need a vacation?

Hard work is healthful, but when a wife is operating on the edge of exhaustion love will sense it, and do something about it.

She May Be Hurting Emotionally

If your wife greets you some evening with a Phyllis Diller hair-do, and a look of total desperation on her face, you can guess that she needs to have some hurts soothed away. She needs to be able to sit down and tell you about the day she's had, which began with her mother calling up and bawling her out for not remembering her birthday, and ended eighteen events later when Jimmy swallowed one of the goldfish.

For a long time I ignored my wife's emotional hurts. They threatened me, because I didn't know what to do about them. I guess I felt that, being a man and the head of the home, if there was a problem, I ought to be able to *do* something about it. And not knowing what to do, I just looked the other way.

Then, one day, a person whom my wife greatly respected said some things to her that were cruelly unkind. I had never seen my wife so deeply hurt.

She was neither angry nor bitter. "I just feel like I want to cry," she said, yet she couldn't. It was like she was numb on the inside.

We were lying side by side in bed. I put my arm around her. For a long time we didn't say anything. After a while we did talk. I don't remember what we said. I just know that somehow we *shared* that hurt.

That is the first need when someone is hurting on the inside. Not "doing" something. Just listening. Understanding. Sharing the hurt.

Afterward you may see some practical things that can be done to correct a situation for the future. But love's first step is to take time to come to where the hurt is.

Some hurts are self-inflicted by an overactive imagination. When a woman is pregnant she may imagine that her husband no longer finds her attractive. Sensing this, he will find special ways to reassure her that she is more than ever "his woman." Reassurance is a healing balm for inner hurt.

When we love we let down our defenses; we expose ourselves. We become vulnerable. The love my wife extends to me exposes her to be hurt by me.

There is truth in the adage, "Those whom we love the most we hurt the most." I love my wife, yet I hurt her. She has entrusted herself to me so completely that she has no defense against my thoughtlessness, my selfishness, my unkindness. More than anyone else, I hurt her. That is the paradox and pain of love.

Having hurt her, I cannot unhurt her. I may resolve not to do it again. If I keep my resolve, it is a solid gain for the marriage, nothing to sneer at. Or I may do something nice to make up for it, which she would genuinely appreciate. But nothing will release healing so simply and so directly as a quiet, "Honey, I was wrong... in doing that. Please forgive me." Only when the waters of forgiveness flow does real healing take place.

Healing does not come from outside. It comes from within the one who has been hurt. A doctor may set a broken arm and put it in a cast, but the power to mend the bone is released from within the person's own body.

We can comfort one who has an inner hurt. We can seek to understand and share the hurt. If we have been the cause of it, we can apologize. But we do not have the power to heal someone else's inner hurt. That power is stored up within the person who has been hurt, in the reservoir of forgiveness. Our listening and comforting and sharing the hurt —even our repentance, when we have caused the hurt—are but love's ways to help release the healing waters.

LOVE COMES TO WHERE THE HURT IS

CHAPTER SEVEN

Sex Should Be Fun

We came at our sexual relationship in a fairly uncomplicated way. We just expected it would be fun—and it was. Today, years later, we still think it is one of the best ideas God ever had.

Our culture extols the high pleasure of sex, and no Victorian hush mutes the message. We discovered, however, that good sex doesn't happen automatically. The pleasure and fulfillment of sex involves more than two people sleeping together in the same bed. When the sexual relationship in marriage is left to just happen, it can as easily lead to frustration and disappointment as to satisfaction. The high pleasure of sex is as much an achievement as it is a discovery.

No advice on the sexual relationship in marriage, we believe, is as practical and profound as two verses in the New Testament. In forty-five words the Apostle Paul captures the essence of an effective sexual relationship. Any couple that will take the time to understand the simple wisdom of these words will open the door to an enrichment of their sexual relationship—

The husband should give to his wife her conjugal rights, and likewise the wife to her husband. For the wife does not rule over her own body, but the husband does; likewise the husband does not rule over his own body, but the wife does.

—1 Corinthians 7:3-4

These words bear on three inter-related dynamics of the sexual relationship: *attitude, atmosphere,* and *action.*

Attitude

The Apostle's point of departure may at first dismay us: The attitude toward the sexual relationship is formed around the controlling concept of *duty.* Not pleasure, not satisfaction, not rights, but duty.

The Apostle recognizes that husband and wife each have marital rights; they have strong urges which need to be satisfied. But this is not what shapes their basic attitude. His word is carefully directed not to the one who has a sexual need, but to the one who has the duty to fulfill it.

The literal meaning in the original Greek is droll: "The husband should pay up on the debt he owes his wife." Some romantic approach! "Well, dear, I managed to scrape together another payment . . . "

What this plain spoken metaphor does, of course, is make vivid a reversal in the natural attitude toward sex—from getting to giving, from attention to my pleasure to attention to my wife's pleasure.

This kind of attitude is typical of Hebrew thought, which focuses not upon human rights but upon human duties. "We teach people to think not in terms of what they demand from others, but of what they owe to others." * According to orthodox Jewish law, the sexual act is the duty of the husband, not his right. Just as it is his duty to provide his wife with food, clothing, and shelter, so he must provide her

---

*"The Jewish Concept of Human Sexuality," Isenstein, Lecture given at *Workshop on Marriage and Family Life Education,* St. John's University, Collegeville, Minnesota, June 1973.

with "oh-nah," which is translated as the conjugal act.

The Apostle Paul makes this fully reciprocal. Husband and wife are mutually 'indebted' to fulfill the sexual needs of the other. It is interesting to note that in other connections Paul recognizes the headship of the husband and the submission of the wife. But in regard to the sexual relation the submission is mutual: The wife has authority over the husband's body and the husband over the wife's.

This is the attitude which needs to control one's approach to the sexual relationship. My mate has a claim upon me, sexually. It is my duty and my privilege to fulfill that claim.

In order to do this I must have some understanding of her expectations, and she of mine. We need to communicate with each other, tell what we like and what we don't like, what excites us and what leaves us cold.

It might be helpful, for instance, if husband and wife were each to describe or even write out a scenario of the sexual act exactly as they would like to experience it, telling the partner what to do from beginning to end. Men and women differ significantly in their sexual responses. We need to help one another understand what we are experiencing in the sexual relationship—what enhances or what detracts from our enjoyment. The more fully we share with one another, the more adequately we can fulfill each other's needs.

Our expectations, of course, must be realistic. By this we do not mean that our expectations should be prosaic, dull, or unimaginative. We mean it in the literal sense: Expectations should focus on the real relationship of husband and wife, not on some impossible "ideal" that we carry around subconsciously.

By the time we marry most of us have acquired a concept of the kind of sexual partner we would like, and the kind of partner we would like to be. It is an ideal pieced together from such varied sources as parental models, teenage fantasy, formal and informal sex education, personal experience of love and affection, romantic novels, peer standards, movies and television, literature, and massive amounts of imagination.

It is not something we consciously work out. It evolves more-or-less spontaneously from the mixture of impressions, ideas, and experiences which we have in regard to sexuality. It can operate in the marriage relationship with powerful effect, often from an unconscious level. Satisfaction with the partner, and with one's own sexual performance, will be measured to some degree in terms of the ideal.

This may not be all bad. Some aspects of the ideal can be worthwhile goals of the sexual relationship. This is especially true where the ideal envisions something for the *relationship* as such, rather than something about the partner.

For instance, the ideal of a statuesque, full-bosomed, Italian movie star type might just as well be set aside if a man has picked for his wife a short, petite woman like his mother. But where one might envision a certain setting for the sexual act—a quiet, unhurried time, with a certain amount of atmosphere, and with many spoken endearments and encouragements—practical steps could be taken to make this kind of an ideal an experienced reality.

My mate's sexual claim upon me is an *exclusive* claim. The commandment against adultery is more than a negative curb on immorality. It is a positive description of the nature of married love.

An actor, well known for his romantic roles, was asked on a television talk show what he considered essential to being a "great lover." His answer, which we cited in the Preface, probably surprised the emcee, but it is an answer every husband should engrave in golden letters and hang in his personal hall of wisdom: "A great lover is someone who can satisfy one woman all her life long, and who can be satisfied by one woman all his life long. A great lover isn't someone who goes from woman to woman to woman. Any dog can do that."

In the sexual relationship one exposes himself at a point of extreme personal vulnerability. A woman risks her femininity, a man his masculinity, in the marriage embrace. But it is that vulnerability, that willingness to expose oneself to the risk of rejection, that opens the door to maturity and fulfillment. A husband who satisfies his wife and is satisfied by her affirms her as a woman. A wife who satisfies her husband and is satisfied by him affirms him as a man.

David du Plessis says, "It takes a wife to make a husband, and a husband to make a wife." Nowhere is this more profoundly expressed than in the sexual relationship.

In every way possible husband and wife should convey to each other, "Your love is delightful. You satisfy me." This needs to come across in words and sighs, in glances and touch, both during love making and at spontaneous and unexpected moments during the day.

It also comes across through *fidelity*. A husband's and wife's faithfulness to one another undergirds all the other ways they tell each other, "I want you, and no one else. You satisfy me."

This attitude is further enhanced when we recognize the spiritual overtones in the sexual relationship. Marriage symbolizes the love of Christ for His Church, the love of God for His people (see Eph. 5:32). That is why Satan hates sex and does everything he can to pervert it. He knows the authority of symbol in spiritual things. Every time a husband and wife come together in marriage they invoke a powerful symbol of love between God and man, a love which Satan has set himself to destroy.

The Bible says, "Rejoice with the wife of your youth" (Prov. 5:18). There is no better antidote to temptation, no better ground for giving growth to a positive attitude toward sex. "This is my woman, the wife God has given me. I will satisfy her. I will delight myself in her."

Atmosphere

Sex is a drama. In a drama the actors move through a series of events toward the destiny or climax envisioned for them by the playwright. The divine Playwright has set before husband and wife the destiny to become one (Gen. 2:24; see also Matt. 19:3-6, Eph. 5:28-32). The sexual encounter is a drama in which they fulfill their God-appointed destiny.

Before a drama begins to move forward, an atmosphere must be created. The background and setting for the action must be established. This will determine the overall style of a drama, and give it a stamp of uniqueness. A single basic plot is capable of many variations. A Greek legend ... became a George Bernard Shaw play ... became "My Fair Lady."

In a survey of married couples which we conducted, 61 percent listed the *setting and mood* as "very important" to their enjoyment of the sexual act, 28 percent felt it was "somewhat important," only 11 percent that it was "not particularly important." There was no significant variation between husbands and wives. Most couples, it would seem, can enter more fully into the drama of sex when the right atmosphere has been created.

By "right atmosphere" we are not suggesting a universal norm. The right atmosphere is the one that is right for a particular couple at a particular time. Most of us, however, could afford to be more imaginative in creating atmosphere for the sexual encounter.

We suggest three basic ingredients that contribute to atmosphere. They can be mixed together with as much variety and innovation as a couple wants: *service, suspense*, and *setting*.

Service

This has to do with the overall atmosphere in the home, the broad "backdrop" for the sexual drama. How do you relate to each other in the normal happenings of married life? How do you speak to one another in the day-to-day routine? A poor scene in the bedroom at 9:30 p.m. may trace back to a thoughtless remark over breakfast coffee.

A frequent complaint voiced by wives goes something like this: "All my husband is interested in is sex." When you pursue that complaint, you discover that usually it does not mean that the wife is uninterested in sex. In some cases she may actually have a stronger sexual appetite than her husband. What the complaint really means is, "I don't like it when the only personal attention I get from my husband is in bed. I want to be more than a sex object."

A woman's sexuality is more diffuse than a man's. For her the atmosphere that supports the sexual encounter must extend beyond the bedroom. She needs to feel herself encircled by her husband's care and commitment in order fully to abandon herself to his sexual embrace.

A man in his early forties once asked me, "What can I do to turn my wife on sexually? She seems completely uninterested in sex."

I knew the man well and had actually been looking for an opportunity to speak to him about his relationship with his wife. I hadn't known about any problem in their sexual relationship until he mentioned it. But I had noticed that when we were together as couples he frequently made jesting slurs about his wife. If it had happened once or twice I would have passed over it as humor. But it was an ingrained habit, and I wondered whether it might indicate a basic attitude that needed to be examined. "Let me be blunt with you," I said. "When you're in the bedroom together, do you ever make fun of her figure or her lovemaking or anything else she does?"

"My God, no!" he exploded. "I do everything I can to encourage her."

"That would be my guess," I told him. "The problem may not be in the bedroom at all. At least it probably doesn't start there."

"You think there's something else—something deeper maybe?"

"Not deeper, really. Just different. Men can compartmentalize sex easier than women. With you it's a question of what happens in the bedroom. With your wife it's a question of your overall relationship. I'd begin by asking myself, 'What kind of a husband am I—outside the bedroom?' I mean things like general courtesy, the way you talk to her, the way you take care of her, the general atmosphere that you create in the home." We went on talking for some time together. I brought up the thing I had noticed, how he made jesting digs at his wife.

At the end he said, "What I hear you telling me is that I need to be a better all-around husband." He laughed, "I came in with one problem, now I've got ten!"

The change was not immediate or dramatic, but he told me about a month later, "Things are going better—in and outside the bedroom!"

Suspense

Like any drama, the drama of sex is heightened when an element of suspense is added.

Many people equate suspense with uncertainty: Suspense is "not knowing what is going to happen next." But in order to have suspense you must focus the uncertainty by introducing a clear note of *prediction* or *intention.* You must tell what is going to happen, or what someone intends to do. That is what creates suspense.

A man who kisses his wife good-bye and says, "Have a nice day," does not create much suspense.

A husband who lets his wife know that he desires her, and intimates his intentions, injects a note of anticipation and suspense into the atmosphere.

"Tonight after dinner I'm going to take the phone off the hook."

"You are?"

"Yes. And then I'm going to build a roaring fire in the fireplace. And I'm going to stretch out on that nice new carpet and watch the flames dance in your eyes."

"You'll have to get close in order to see them."
"I'm going to."
"And if I close my eyes?"
"Then I'll get closer still. . ."

Sometimes, when husband and wife sense a desire for each other, but the time or situation does not allow it, a promise of "tonight . . ." or "when I get back . . ." can add a winsome expectancy to the atmosphere. If a man is away from home, he can introduce an element of anticipation by something he writes in a letter.

Of course the sexual encounter is often delightful when it is spontaneous and unplanned. But both husband and wife can afford to vary this by bringing in an element of suspense from time to time. Anticipation adds a particular kind of enjoyment to the sexual relationship. It can also help the woman, whose sexual arousal is slower and more subtle than the man's, come to the encounter more eager and responsive.

Setting

The most common setting for the sexual encounter is a) at night, b) in bed. It is the time and the place most convenient and natural for most couples.

Slight changes in this standard setting can enhance the encounter. You might experiment with the lighting. Making love in the dark heightens the sense of touch. But the encounter can also be enhanced by visual stimulation. One man said that he and his wife especially enjoyed making love by candlelight.

What you wear is also part of the setting, and can be varied, sometimes with startling effect. One woman, at the suggestion of a marriage counselor, came into the bedroom wearing a fur coat and high heels—and nothing else. Her husband was already in his pajamas, sitting on the edge of the bed.

"What's up?" he asked innocently. "Aren't you coming to bed?"

"I am," she said, slipping out of her heels as she walked toward him.

The next morning as he was leaving for work he said, "Hey, that fur coat routine—that was something else!" A week later *he* came into the bedroom—dressed like a pirate!

They both concluded that their sexual relationship had become dull, and these little episodes helped to lighten the atmosphere.

"At first I thought it was silly," the wife said, "but we both enjoyed it, so who cares?"

That is the essential criterion: Do both husband and wife enjoy it? Does it add to their sense of fun and pleasure? Does it refresh the relationship?

The standard setting may be perfectly satisfactory most of the time. But from time to time you will both enjoy a touch of variety. A different time of day. A different place. A provocative nightgown.

One last word about the setting. It must be *securely private.* The wife, especially, cannot abandon herself to the sexual encounter if she fears being intruded upon. A lock on the bedroom door is a wise investment for successful sex.

Action

Traditionally men have been regarded as "active" in the sexual relationship, women as "passive." Current Christian literature on sex is fairly consistent in urging the wife to take a more active role in the relationship. A survey of 100,000 women by *Redbook* magazine indicated that women, especially those who consider themselves "religious," are active partners in the sexual relationship. This is a wholesome corrective of the image of a wife as a passive, silently enduring martyr.

There is a sense, however, in which the traditional roles are still helpful in understanding the dynamics of the sexual relationship. The *Redook* survey indicated that even though wives are active partners in the relationship, the sexual encounter is still *initiated* by husbands the majority of the time. Our own research, which included both husbands and wives, indicated this even more strongly. This appears to be true in all age brackets and simply reflects a universal characteristic of the man-woman relationship: The man is usually the initiator, the woman the responder.

Putting these two factors together, we could describe the woman's participation as *actively-passive*, i.e., she is an *active responder*.

"I want to make love *with* my wife, not to her," said one husband. "I want her to respond to me, hold me, kiss me, fondle me. When we start making love I don't want her to just lie there. I want her to respond."

In her book, *The Total Woman*, Marabel Morgan writes, "A woman's hands should never be still when she is making love. By caressing tenderly, you assure him that he's touchable. Tell him 'I love you' with your hands." That's a good picture of an active responder.

The man, on the other hand, could be described as *passively-active*, i.e., he is a *responsive initiator*. As the lovemaking gets under way, he must be sensitive to his wife's needs and desires. He must key his actions to her rising response.

In counseling young couples for marriage we usually suggest that they read a good book on the sexual relationship. *The Freedom of Sexual Love* by Harry and Lois Bird, and *The Act of Marriage* by Tim and Beverly La Haye are excellent. (We do not agree with all of the La Hayes' advice concerning *contraception*. They recommend methods which we believe can detract from the fullest meaning and experience of the sexual relationship. Two methods which they recommend can be dangerous to the woman—the pill and the IUD. We appreciate their non-permissive attitude toward abortion, though their handling of specific cases leaves some important questions unanswered, e.g., the effect of abortion on future child-bearing possibilities. These issues, however, take up only a small part of their book, which otherwise is one of the most helpful that has been written.)

In addition to recommending books, we go on to tell couples, "You yourselves will be the best teachers of one another."

No book can tell a husband what pleases a woman as precisely as can his own wife—if she is willing to communicate. Books can give general guidelines for lovemaking. The wife must help make her husband a lover.

Successful sex depends in considerable measure on how willing husband and wife are to instruct one another.

Kay Arthur, popular lecturer on the marriage relationship, said in one of her talks, "When you go to bed with your husband, make sure you enjoy it. Don't just lie there and endure. Make it fun. It's important for your husband to know that he satisfies you. That's why you have to share with him *how* to satisfy you.

"Don't lie there and fume to yourself, 'Why doesn't this dumb man know how to turn me on? Why doesn't he know what to do?'

"That is the way I felt. My ego held me back from telling him what to do to turn me on. (What if he resented it?) So I'd weep, and suffer, and feel sorry for myself because I didn't get turned on.

"Then one day I got up my courage and told him how. I told him what to do to turn me on. I was scared, but I did it. And . . . oh boy! I quit suffering! It became very satisfying.

"And *he* was happier. He had the feeling, 'Look how I've satisfied her.' Because his desire was not just to be satisfied himself, but also to satisfy me. There's something in them that wants to know, 'I can satisfy her.' "

What turns a woman on? Well, put your ego out on a limb and ask her! She'll probably give you some ideas you never got out of books or locker rooms.

Men like to give the impression that knowledge about things sexual is something they mastered a long time ago. It would be humiliatingly pre-adolescent to admit to any significant gaps in their understanding of how to go about making love to a woman. When you see this attitude already surfacing in unmarried sixteen-year-olds, and persisting virtually unchanged with married men into middle age, you begin to suspect that male sexual bravado probably covers over the greatest concentration of mass ignorance in the human encyclopedia.

One of the homework assignments we give couples in our family life seminars is to write down specific things they like or don't like in their sexual relationship, and then to discuss this with one another. Couples have written to us afterward and said that "discussing those eight questions opened up a new chapter in our sex life . . .''

1. Are there two things which my mate does that especially please or satisfy me during sexual relations? (When we're doing something right, we should be encouraged to continue!)

2. Is there one thing which my mate does in our sexual relations which I do not particularly like or enjoy? (Explain briefly why you don't like or enjoy it.)

3. When or how do I get the most pleasure out of our sexual relations?

4. What do I do which seems to give my mate the most pleasure in our sexual relations?

5. Is there something I like, which my mate does not seem to like or respond to?

6. How often do I like to have sexual relations? How often does my mate seem to want sexual relations?

7. When do I most like to have sexual relations? When least?

8. What do I like best about our sexual relations? What least?

In a survey we conducted, one thing we suggested was for husband and wife each to write a brief scenario "in which you tell your mate exactly how you would like to experience an act of loveplay and intercourse, giving specific instructions as to what would make it enjoyable for you."

Some couples find it more difficult than others to verbalize their ideas and desires. That does not mean they cannot instruct one another. The communication that takes place during the sexual encounter, much of it non-verbal, can gently direct the mate to do those things that please and satisfy—sighs, whispers, guiding the hands, bodily movements. However it is communicated, husbands and wives need to let each other know exactly what they want. Only in this way can they do what they are committed to do, and what each deeply wants to do, and that is truly to serve one another, to bring the mate to the point of complete sexual fulfillment and satisfaction.

Husbands and Wives, TEACH ONE ANOTHER TO LOVE

CHAPTER EIGHT

Contraception: Blessing or Blight?

"My fiancee and I have read through The Christian Family * *as part of our preparation for getting married. But we have a question which is not dealt with in the book. What about* contraception? *Do you or your wife have any views on the subject?"*

Dear Friend,

Thank you for your letter, telling your experience of reading *The Christian Family.* It is interesting that you should ask about our views on contraception. Larry and I have only recently come to the conclusion that we should share our views on this subject.

More and more people are coming to see the importance of this question, though as Protestants we have discussed it very little. Virtually all couples today recognize the need for limiting the number of children they have. It is difficult to raise a large family in our society.

When we were married in 1951, we didn't consider very deeply or seriously how to limit our family. We probably started out like most Protestant couples of that era. I went to the doctor for a premarital exam and was fitted with a contraceptive device.

---

* *The Christian Family* by Larry Christenson. Bethany Fellowship, Inc., Minneapolis, Minnesota, 1970. 216 pp.

We knew we wanted to have children. We knew we wanted to limit the number of children. No one in our acquaintance raised any questions about contraception. In fact, no one had ever suggested to us that there was any other way to live. We had heard that Catholics weren't cued in to this, but we thought that was merely an idiosyncrasy. It never occurred to us, being a modern married couple, that there was any other way than to use some kind of contraceptive.

Many other couples have undoubtedly started marriage in the same way, never feeling that there was any alternative. In some cases, because of economic reasons, health factors, or other limitations their plans probably had to be even more stringent than ours.

Later we came to feel that our experience with commonly used contraceptives was not entirely satisfactory. Evidently we weren't alone in this. Walter and Ingrid Trobisch, an Austrian Lutheran pastor and his wife, known worldwide for their teaching and counseling on human sexuality say, "When talking to couples in Europe and America, we discovered that many were ill at ease with the methods offered to them in dealing with their fertility. If the proposed methods of conception control were as safe and as satisfying in their application as is often claimed, the problem of unwanted pregnancies should actually no longer exist." [1]

After twelve years we decided we would no longer use a contraceptive device. We had encountered no special problem in using it, but I had come to detest the sense of intrusion it brought into our relationship. Up until this time only one person had suggested to me that it was possible to avoid conception without the use of a contraceptive device—Dr. Konald Prem, a Catholic obstetrician who had been very helpful to me during a difficult pregnancy. He later became chairman of the Department of Obstetrics and Gynecology at the University of Minnesota Medical School. He said there were natural means of planning and spacing a family.

He exerted no pressure on me to accept a natural method, merely stating that he and his wife knew from personal experience that pregnancy could be avoided without the use of contraception. I valued his opinion, but several years went by before I came to the conclusion that "there must be a better way" than contraception. It was then that we decided to try the calendar rhythm method (not the same as the currently taught methods of natural family planning).

I became pregnant the first month! That was not much encouragement for this new step. The failure, however, was not the fault of the system; I learned that I had calculated incorrectly. In spite of my mistake, we didn't go back to the contraceptive, which in retrospect is a little amazing. I think we had simply "had it" with artificial contraceptives and were not going to be easily discouraged. (This pregnancy miscarried. Though it had been unplanned, we were disappointed.)

The calendar rhythm method, like all other natural methods, is based on the fact that although a man's fertility is nearly constant day after day, a woman's fertility is limited to a brief period each menstrual cycle. Larry and I have used this method, refraining from intercourse during the fertile period, since 1963. Once I learned to count correctly, it worked fine!

During these years I had one other pregnancy;

like the previous one it miscarried so our family doesn't include these children. But the pregnancy itself was no fault of the system. I had gone so long without a pregnancy that I began wishfully thinking, "I'm getting so old, there's no need to count these days anymore!" It was very clear to us that when we avoided intercourse during the fertile days there was no pregnancy; when we paid no attention to the cycle, I got pregnant.

That is a very matter-of-fact account of our experience. But the personal dimensions of it go much deeper than a mere, "We can avoid pregnancy." We believe that the years have confirmed and rewarded us in our decision to stop using a contraceptive device. Our sexual relationship has developed in a new way. We love and delight in each other more. Sexuality has become a more enjoyable, natural part of my life. We attribute this to our discovery of natural family planning. I would not go back to using a contraceptive device even if the alternative were having twenty-one children.

This experience has led us to wonder what the consequences of using contraception might be on other marriages. We know contraception prevents pregnancy rather effectively. It is much easier to see that than to ascertain what else it might do. Could contraception be a contributing factor to the immature, unsatisfying sex life which marriage counselors hear about and divorce statistics confirm? Is contraception an unsuspected blight on modern marriage?

Larry and I feel that couples should be warned against the *unthinking acceptance* of contraceptives. Every married couple should come to their decision based on the best physiological, psychological, and scriptural knowledge. We believe that natural family planning offers distinct advantages over the use of mechanical or chemical contraceptives. It is a viable option which merits serious consideration.

I wonder what we are really saying to ourselves when we prepare for this most intimate act by donning contraceptive machinery or by negating the act chemically? Can we treat ourselves like machines, closing off an undesirable valve and expecting the rest of the machine to operate smoothly? As persons we are a profound union of many components which are subtly interrelated and interdependent. We are much more than a biological machine.

Father Charles Curran, the theologian who led the opposition to Pope Paul's encyclical *Humanae Vitae,* forbidding the use of contraception, criticized the Pope for taking a simplistic, too-biological view of intercourse. But that is precisely an argument *against* contraception. The use of contraceptives presupposes that a mere physical prevention of conception is all that occurs. We think that nothing else is affected, that the psychology of sex, the intimate relationship, and the marriage itself remain untouched. Is not *this* the simplistic, too-biological view of human nature and of the sex act?

Our actions speak more forcefully to our deep mind than do our intellectual rationalizations. Do we set up a conflict within ourselves when we attempt to say with one action, "I want to be one with you," while with another action we imply, "I reject the possible consequences of this oneness"? One intelligent, cultured, internationally traveled woman said to me in Mexico City that she felt she had suffered mental illness while taking the pill because of a schizophrenic division of sexuality from personality.

A busy educated couple in England described to us their utter frustration and non-enjoyment in the experience of sexual intercourse. Yet they seemed to sense no connection between this attitude and the fact that they felt a pregnancy would be the ultimate catastrophe. Is this *marriage*? When avoiding pregnancy claims the first priority in our sexual relationship a distortion is created that can warp the whole marriage relationship.

What is marriage? We need to come back to basics. The nature of marriage includes sexual intercourse. The nature of sexual intercourse includes the possibility of pregnancy.

Although the contraceptive mentality tends to play this down, no contraceptive method is an absolute guarantee that sexual intercourse will not result in pregnancy. The contraceptive mentality leads us to believe that intercourse without pregnancy is our right, a right all but guaranteed by modern science. The "failure rate" to which every type of contraceptive admits will involve someone else, certainly not *us*. (I appreciate the comment of John and Sheila Kippley that when a contraceptive fails to prevent conception the result is not a "failure" but a *human being*.) [2]

The contraceptive mentality says that we have the right to sexual intercourse and also the right to reject the fruit of this relationship and act. When we accept contraception we open the door to more and more drastic steps to prevent or annihilate pregnancy. At least this has been the history of the last fifty years. The right to reject the consequences of intercourse is not given us by nature. There is no natural way that we can experience the sex act without the possibility of pregnancy. That is one part of our earthly life over which God has not given us dominion.

The contraceptive mentality begins by saying, "We cannot (will not, must not, should not) have a baby." If, contrary to our expectation, conception occurs, then abortion could be the next logical step. We have a *right* to expect that the contraceptive will work, and if it doesn't, it's not *our* fault, is it?

Who can measure the unhappiness brought on by such manipulation and rationalization? We are deceiving ourselves if we think that we can accept the privilege of sexual intercourse but turn our backs on responsibility toward the fruit of our action.

Much of the rationalization for both contraception and abortion says that they are required because of the tremendous problems faced by families and by society. But if to solve problems we deny the integrity and responsibility for our actions, we only precipitate other problems—perhaps not immediately apparent, but even deeper. John Kippley says it well: "Man should respond to the challenges of life in ways that are not destructive of authentic human values." [3]

What I have described is the essence of a mentality pervasive in our society. I am not suggesting that every person who uses contraception would favor or resort to abortion. I do say, however, that the two ideas—(1) we have a right to sexual intercourse, and (2) we have a right not to get pregnant—are fundamentally incompatible and invite serious marital and social problems.

Are there attitudes which carry over from non-acceptance of pregnancy to the children one already has or to children in general? Does the contraceptive mentality develop those instincts of motherhood and fatherhood needed for happy families? The Bible says children are a precious gift, a heritage of the Lord. It has become easy in our time to regard them as an annoyance and an inconvenience. Our society does not honor and value children, and the message is certainly coming across to the children. Our material accomplishments and acquisitions often claim a higher priority. What will these priorities yield us in later life—reward or regret?

Elizabeth Kübler-Ross, who has done much research on death and dying, was asked if her work with dying people had changed her. She answered, "If I were to lose this house and everything in it, I couldn't care less. If you listen to dying patients say, 'If only I had gotten to know my children. If only . . . ' you begin to reflect on your own life." [4] We need to reflect on the priorities we establish in our marriages.

The anti-baby attitude is growing. More and more young couples are rejecting the center of life: having a family and experiencing the irreplaceable opportunity of growing up with children. Some beautiful young people request sterilization determined never to have children. Others hand their infants over for someone else to raise and to influence their formation. What remorse will such decisions yield later on?

It is my experience and suspicion that the use of contraceptives dampens a woman's enthusiasm, hinders her complete involvement in the act of intercourse, and therefore may arrest her whole sexual development. When the intimacy of marriage is interrupted physically or psychologically, it is possible that it will be more difficult for her to accept it as a good and natural gift of God.

The sexual relationship, like the rest of our being, should grow, develop, deepen, and mature through the years. Isn't it possible that contraception arrests this development because of its unnatural approach to intercourse? Rather than accepting intercourse as a unity, an upbuilding act which binds together, we seek to isolate the thrilling, soaring experience and enjoy only that. Could we ever say, for example, to a plant, "Give me only the beautiful red flower; never mind about the roots, the foliage, the fruit"? The plant without maturing roots and foliage will not flower. Would a society at peace and content with its sexuality be so preoccupied with sex? Perhaps our sex-obsessed society is the result of so little real sexual fulfillment. Are we seeking sex more often and enjoying it less because of the widespread use of contraceptives?

Most couples have had little or no opportunity to choose a natural method. General information about the practicality and joys of natural family planning is not readily available, because the scientific and medical communities have largely chosen to ignore this possibility. Every hospital is required to have information available on family planning. Since there is a growing openness toward natural family planning, especially among younger couples, some hospitals are providing information about it as an option for married couples. Some local associations also provide teaching and encouragement to couples who want to use a natural method. The Couple-to-Couple League, a national organization of married couples, helps other couples learn natural family planning. Its publication, *The Art of Natural Family*

Planning by John and Sheila Kippley, is an excellent handbook on the philosophy and implementation of natural methods.

Many people believe as we did that natural methods are a Catholic idiosyncracy. But we have talked with both Protestant and Jewish couples whose experience parallels our own. A Los Angeles research project on natural family planning, funded by the Department of Health, Education and Welfare, attracted more non-Catholic than Catholic volunteers in 1976. We owe a debt of gratitude to the Catholics, who for years have taken a stand against contraception as being unworthy of marriage. It seems to us that they have helped point us to a better way.

A growing number of couples are beginning to reconsider the advisability of contraception. Young couples, learning about the possible side effects from taking the pill—increased risk of blood clots in the legs, lungs, and brain; heart attacks, high blood pressure; blindness; cancer; liver dysfunction; fetal deformities—are deciding that these are not risks they wish to take. Another effect of the pill which is now coming to light is that fertility sometimes does not return when the medication is discontinued, as was promised.

Dr. Kevin Hume of Australia has said, "Twenty years ago we got the good news about the pill." The good news was that research scientists had developed a medication which would suppress ovulation (the release of the egg from the ovary), and therefore prevent conception. The pill was hailed as the perfect contraceptive. The woman took it about three weeks out of every four. Since she did this at a time not associated with sexual intercourse, it eliminated the ugly interruption of the love scene required by some other forms of contraception. Dr. Hume continued, "All the news since then has been bad news."

Anyone who mentions the bad news is accused of peddling "horror stories." The risks cited above, however, are not fabrications of an irresponsible alarmist: they come from a longer list published by a pharmaceutical company which manufactures the pill, warning doctors to discontinue the medication at the first sign of any of these maladies.

Women have a right to full information about the risks of medications they are taking. Only belatedly is information about the side effects of the pill being made available to the women who take it. Women who expressed misgivings about long-time interference with the reproductive mechanism were often patted on the head and told that there was nothing to worry about.

There was a great stir to ban saccharin from the market because in massive doses it tended to produce cancer in mice. For years the pill has produced catastrophic results, not in experimental animals but in women. Yet one hears little or no suggestion that it be banned. An objective evaluation of this situation surely substantiates Kippley's assertion that "there are strong forces that work toward diminished moral vision when it comes to birth control." [5]

Some medical authorities have rationalized the use of the pill, saying that it is "safer than pregnancy." Admittedly there are risks to the mother's health in pregnancy, although these are minimized by adequate care. But must we say the obvious? Pregnancy is necessary if the human race is to continue. The health risks involved in taking the pill are unnecessary. There are better ways of limiting the number of children in a family, ways that are not dangerous to the mother. To say that pregnancy is as dangerous as the pill implies that pregnancy and the pill are equally dispensable. Here is an example of the crass anti-baby propaganda under which we live.

The IUD (intrauterine device) is another method of contraception recommended because of its high rate of effectiveness and because it does not need to be inserted right at the time of sexual intercourse. It has, however, serious implications for the woman's health.

The IUD is a flexible plastic or metal device which a doctor inserts into the woman's uterus. Some are shaped like loops, bows, or irregularly shaped discs, some like a metal umbrella frame. The exact way the IUD works is not obvious. Dr. Thomas Hilgers says that the IUD "creates a hostile milieu for the zygote." [6] That means that the IUD does not prevent conception (the joining of the egg with the male sperm), but that when the fertilized egg (zygote) arrives in the uterus the IUD prevents the implantation of the zygote which is then expelled. Because the IUD does not prevent fertilization of the egg it is not a contraceptive. It causes an early abortion and therefore must be classified as an abortifacient.

Human life is a continuous development from conception to natural death, and so the use of the IUD raises serious moral problems. (The pill presents us with this problem also. The effect of the pill is such that if ovulation does take place and conception occurs, the lining of the uterus is modified, making it less favorable for implantation.) [7]

Beside the moral implication of the IUD, there are serious health factors to be considered. The long-range effects of this chronic inflammation of the lining of the uterus are not yet known. It is known, however, that it has caused infection in the pelvic organs resulting in sterility in some women. Women have had the IUD puncture the wall of the uterus and migrate into the body cavity requiring a surgical procedure for removal. Should pregnancy occur with an IUD in place (and it does) removal of the IUD may cause an abortion.

The IUD and the pill support the idea, "Avoid pregnancy at all costs." What they do to the woman's health and well-being has been overlooked. There is more to be considered about a contraceptive than that it prevents pregnancy and does not interfere with the marriage embrace.

If you feel that you should avoid pregnancy, it is possible to do so by natural means. Natural methods are based on the scientific fact that a woman's fertility is limited to a short time each menstrual cycle when the ovum (egg) is released from the ovary. When the couple abstain from intercourse for a few days around the time of ovulation, conception does not take place.

Calendar rhythm was the pioneer method of natural family planning. It is based on the research of Dr. Kyusaku Ogino (1930) in Japan and of Dr. Herman Knaus (1929), working independently in Austria. Their research "discovered that a woman ovulates (is fertile) about two weeks before the beginning of her next menstrual period. In the years since then, much additional information has been discovered about the changes that occur in a woman's body during the fertile part of her monthly cycle. No one seriously involved in natural family planning today recommends the use of the Ogino-Knaus rhythm, and the criticisms of it do not apply to the methods taught today. At the same time, it should be recognized that the Ogino-Knaus rhythm could be effective for about 80 percent of married couples if they were willing to abide by its rules." [8]

Contrary to what is sometimes said about calendar rhythm, it does not require perfect regularity in the length of cycles. Its main weakness is that it is based on previous menstrual history and cannot adjust to any unexpected variation in the present cycle. Another flaw is the prolonged abstinence imposed when cycles vary greatly in length. Further medical research has identified physical signs which accompany ovulation and therefore enable the woman to assess her fertility on a current basis:

(1) At about the time of ovulation the woman's waking temperature rises from lower to a higher level, which is then sustained until the next menstrual period begins.

(2) A cervical mucus appears during the fertile period and ovulation pain may occur.

(3) It is possible to monitor changes in the height, consistency, and openness of the cervix (the lower part of the uterus) indicating different phases of the cycle.

The Sympto-Thermic method of natural family planning teaches the observation and interpretation of these three signs to determine the approach, presence, and passing of the fertile time. Couples can choose to abstain from intercourse at this time, thereby avoiding pregnancy, or they can use it to achieve pregnancy.

Another method refined and taught by Drs. John and Lyn Billings, an Australian husband-wife team, depends entirely on reading the mucus sign. This Ovulation (mucus) Method is easy and effective for many couples, predicting the approach of ovulation even when cycles are of irregular length. It can be used while breastfeeding or during pre-menopause, when no other method is practical.

Some women find it difficult to interpret the mucus sign and therefore feel more confident using the Sympto-Thermic combination of signs. Dr. Lyn Billings recommends, however, that a woman first learn to read the mucus sign so that she can acquire confidence in it.

I know that it is possible for a woman to be perfectly secure and at ease in using a natural method of family planning if she obtains good instruction and gives herself time to gain experience. I have had this experience myself and have talked with many other experienced women. If a young woman takes the time and effort to learn the meaning of the different signs of fertility (ideally she should begin to do this several months before marriage), it will serve her well until the menopause.

The natural methods involve no risk to a woman's health. They enhance her understanding and appreciation of her bodily functions and allow her to live in harmony with her womanhood. They support the biblical concept of a woman's body being "fearfully and wonderfully made" (Ps. 119:14)—an instrument created by God, complex yet capable of being understood. They treat fertility as a precious gift of God, to be loved, respected, understood and wisely used. They "leave the sexual embrace in its natural beauty." [9] They also have a high rate of effectiveness when they are used correctly. They depend upon an intelligent perception of the approach of the fertile period and abstinence from sexual intercourse during that time.

The feature of abstinence causes some couples to doubt the practicality of natural methods. They say things like—

"We would lose the spontaneity in our love life. How can that be natural?"

"We would live in constant fear of pregnancy."

"How can it be good to abstain from intercourse on certain days of every cycle."

"My husband would never stand for that. I am afraid he would be tempted to unfaithfulness if I denied him."

However, satisfied husbands say things like—

"Life is sweet living with a natural method."

"It's like the honeymoon when we come back together."

"Our sex life has blossomed in a new and even more satisfying way."

"It works!"

The abstinence shouldn't be looked upon as a "no love" time, but rather as a time when husband and wife express love in other ways. One couple described it as "a courtship and honeymoon every month."

We have been brainwashed into thinking that the worst thing we can do is impose any kind of restraint on our sexual desire. But sexual restraint is a normal part of life. Chastity before marriage and fidelity in marriage requires sexual restraint. Everyone must practice sexual self-denial unless he wants to end up in the gutter.

Denying ourselves sexual expression is not dangerous. Denying that we have sexual feelings is unhealthy. But unless we sink into self-pity, saying No to the expression of these feelings is not harmful to oneself or one's marriage.

Abstinence is not always easy. It can be a physical pain to deny yourself. But in the morning the pain is gone, whereas a pregnancy would continue.

What price are we willing to pay to avoid having too large a family? Our society says, "Don't accept the price of self-denial; let someone else pay the bill."

Permissive, undisciplined life has the green light in our time. It is unpopular to suggest things like abstinence, self-denial. But someone always ends up paying the bill. We pass it on to our mate, our marriage, our children, our unborn, our community. And in the end we ourselves do not escape. We pay a cost that can be staggering in terms of unfulfilled dreams, emptiness, and broken families and relationships.

It is time to consider again the value of self-denial. It has been the witness of saints thoughout the ages that self-denial, by the grace of God, does not impoverish but rather enriches us. And this has been our experience. Periods of sexual abstinence refresh and renew the relationship.

It needs to be said that a married couple has the freedom to choose not to abstain. That is one of the privileges of marriage. But when a couple chooses not to abstain during the fertile period, they should accept the possibility of pregnancy. In our view this is a responsibility to which we commit ourselves in marriage.

One day I said to our sixteen-year-old son that a young man should not entertain thoughts of getting married until he can support a wife and child. His surprised answer: "He shouldn't?" This idea was completely new to him. The commonly accepted norm is that young people get married whenever they want to and plan that the woman's wage-earning power will continue as long as they want it to. They do not seriously consider the possibility of a child coming along to change this plan. With this attitude, is it any wonder that pregnancy rather than being the cause for joy and congratulations, which it ought to be, becomes the occasion for disappointment, bitterness, and unhappiness? Children belong to the nature of marriage. How much happier young couples would be if they accepted this as primary in marriage.

It is important that a couple be in agreement about avoiding conception by using a method based on fertility awareness. One partner cannot do it alone. This marriage-building factor in the natural methods strengthens a couple's communication and unites them in making this important decision and plan.

The husband has the greater responsibility in accepting the periodic abstinence. If it is to his advantage to limit the number of children in the family, it is to his advantage to take the lead in abstinence, rejecting self-pity, supporting his wife, and expressing affection in other ways during her fertile days. This attitude can make the marriage stronger, more beautiful, and deeply satisfying for both husband and wife.

We recommend that couples once again accept the entirety of the marriage act and the full truth of their relationship: that they either limit their family's size through periodic abstinence based on fertility awareness or else adopt a life-style compatible with a larger family. In other words, let us take responsibility for our actions—or not act.

We hope our views and the information we have given will help you to make a more informed decision about dealing with your fertility. We pray God's blessing on your marriage.

Sincerely,
Nordis Christenson

Acknowledgment

We gratefully acknowledge the help of the following people who read this chapter, made suggestions, and checked it for scientific accuracy: Virginia Gager, Sarasota, Florida; John Kippley, Cincinnati, Ohio; and Konald Prem, M.D., Chairman, Department of Obstetrics and Gynecology, University of Minnesota Medical School, Minneapolis, Minnesota.

"FEARFULLY AND WONDERFULLY MADE"

CHAPTER NINE

Obedience, the Doorway to Love

When Steve and Joyce fell in love it was no light tumble, more like an avalance. They could stand in the middle of a jostling crowd, holding hands, and see and hear nothing but each other. The longing way they looked into each other's eyes, oblivious to all else, prompted one old-timer to say, "Like two dying calves in a snowstorm. They'd better get married and end the misery."

They had been married two years when they came to see me. They said they were having some "problems." After several minutes of hemming and hawing Joyce dropped her face into her hands and sobbed.

"He says he doesn't love me anymore."

Steve shrugged his shoulders helplessly, as though she had let fall the verdict of terminal illness over his life.

"I don't know—" he stammered. "I just don't feel the same toward her anymore."

What can you do when you feel differently toward your wife? You begin to notice little things about her that irritate you. You have no desire to hold her in your arms. Sex is routine. You don't enjoy talking with her. You don't look forward to coming home at night. When she tries to get close to you, you stiffen up. Love has cooled.

I told them I didn't think they were as bad off as they thought they were. They looked at me surprised, glancing sideways at each other.

"Let me read you something I said to you when I married you." I took out the short wedding sermon by Dietrich Bonhoeffer that I usually include in the wedding liturgy, and read them this sentence: "It is not your love that sustains marriage, but from now on it is your marriage that will sustain your love."

They had experienced love as an attraction and an emotion. I began to talk with them about love as an expression of the *will*.

Love's Source

The love I have for my wife does not originate with me. It originates with God, and comes to me in the form of a command: *Husband, love your wife.*

The love that is in the heart of God flows into human marriage through this word addressed to the will of the husband. When I obey that word, there is released in our marriage the same supernatural love with which Christ loves the church.

Obey ... and love. This is the strength of Christian marriage. It does not expect to sustain itself on the seasonal streams of our own feelings. It draws water from the deep well of Christ's love, which never runs dry. The quality of love which we experience in marriage depends upon how open we are to the inflow of this word of Christ.

Christ addresses His word to our will because the will is the doorkeeper of our life. It stands guard at the door named obedience and determines what shall come in. When the will puts its hand to obedience, it opens up our life to the authority and power of the word which stands waiting on the threshold.

It is no small responsibility which the Creator

has entrusted to the will, for many a traveler comes knocking at this door! Family, Society, Self-will, the Philosophies of Culture, Emissaries of Temptation, the Voice of Duty, Wisdom and Knowledge in varied garb, the *Zeitgeist* ("the spirit of the times"), Education, Impulses, Possessions—friends, enemies, authorities, benefactors, quacks, and charlatans— all clamoring for access to our lives. And in the press of all that throng stands Christ, waiting His turn to knock and seek entrance into a life which He himself has created and redeemed. Love clad in patience. Humility that shames us to speechless wonder.

When the word of Christ comes to the threshold of our lives, the will must reach out and take a firm grip on the doorknob of obedience. When the word is, "Husbands, love your wives," turning the knob and swinging open the door will mean some practical demonstration of love toward my wife.

"Write down on a slip of paper three things your wife would like you to do," I said to Steve.

I handed him a slip of paper and a pencil. After a few moments he shrugged and turned the question to Joyce. "What do you want me to do?" She was still upset and only shrugged back. He sat a while longer staring at the paper. And then something seemed to happen inside him. His will slowly reached out and took hold of the doorknob. He started writing, slowly at first, then more quickly. He handed the paper back to me, and the hint of a smile traced across his face. I had asked for three things, he wrote down five—

Hang up my clothes when I undress at night
Be nice to her brother
Sit with my arm around her when we watch TV

Talk more
Take her out sometimes

"Are these things you feel you could to?" I asked.
"I guess so."

I numbered the items to suggest a priority of 1-3-2-5-4 and handed the slip back to him. "Okay, you've written your own assignment. Try doing them in the order I've suggested. Add to the list if you want to."

"I don't want him to love me because he has to," Joyce said plaintively. "I want him to love me because he wants to."

"Your love is entering a new phase," I said. "To begin with it was supported by strong feeling and emotion. Now it needs to be undergirded by the will. Believe me, you'll discover a new dimension to love, and it won't be without feeling either."

Neither one of them looked too happy, but they left with the promise to meet with me again in two weeks. Little did we realize that God had enrolled all three of us in a "school" that would last more than five years.

I had spoken glibly about exercising the will. That was a bare skeleton of the truth. It took on flesh and blood only as God patiently unfolded to us the critical role that *faith* plays in the whole process.

Love's Direction

Joyce had expressed a commonly held idea, the notion that love is not genuine unless it wells up spontaneously out of the feelings. The will can only ratify the feelings. It cannot initiate or direct any expression of love. "He must love me because he wants to, not because he has to." More simply put:

"I don't want him to love me unless he feels like it."

Ideally love will engage and be expressed through both feelings and will. But sometimes a conflict arises between the two. And then it is a question of *which one shall take the lead?*

A man who was genuinely devoted to his wife was sent by his company on a three-week assignment to audit the accounts of a subsidiary in another state. Within a week an attractive woman in the office made it plain that she was available for an after-hours relationship. He found himself drawn to her, no denying it. He lay awake most of one night wrestling with his conscience. His feelings would have impelled him one way, but his will held back, reticent to accept the rationalizations his mind was concocting. In the end he decided to remain faithful to his wife. Not because he "wanted to" (a very real part of him "wanted" to have a fling with the other woman), but because he *willed* to express his love to his wife by being faithful to her.

One of the Big Lies of our culture is that we cannot say No to our feelings. Some counter-propaganda is needed. Unless we *do* say some well-chosen No's to our feelings, we will make a shamble of our lives, most certainly of our marriages.

Joyce's concern needed to be put in a much larger frame. "I want him to love me because—" Only because he "wants to"? Only because he feels a certain way? The feelings form one part of the background. The rest of the picture needs to be brought into view: "I want him to love me because—

> he is my husband
> we have pledged our lives to each other

> we are bound together by God's Word and by our
> vows
> he is the father of our child
> we are accountable for our life together before
> God and men."

To live responsibly is a large part of what it means to be a man. When a man marries he makes a solemn vow to love his wife for no other reason than that she is his wife. If he behaves like a man, he does not subject that vow to the caprice of undisciplined feelings, for if he did the love would never mature. Indeed, the feelings themselves would become stunted and misshapen. He makes his love subject to the Word of God and to the marriage vow. He roots his will deep in the soil of obedience.

From this can grow a love which will not get uprooted by every passing wind of feeling and go tumbleweeding all over the landscape. It will develop a strong root structure. It will send up sturdy branches. It will be able to survive dry spells. It will produce healthy fruit, including feelings that are both tender and passionate; feelings that have found their rightful place, which is not to direct love but to enhance it.

Such love is no cause for lament. On the contrary, a woman so loved by her husband should exult: "Thank God, I am loved by a *man*!"

Love's Power

If obedience opens our life to Christ, it is faith that invites Him in. Already in the act of obedience, of course, faith is at work. When I swing open the door of my house to someone whose voice I recognize, I do it because I trust him; I have come to have faith in the kind of person he is. But the next thing

I do is invite him in. And then faith becomes more specific. I don't just trust him in a general way for the kind of person he is. My faith focuses upon the purpose of this particular visit.

When Christ stands at the threshold of your life and says, "Husband, love your wife," He wants obedience. Not for its own sake. That would be like a man coming to your house and knocking just so he could watch you open doors. He wants obedience because He wants access to your life. Obedience is the door through which you let Him in.

There is, then, a double action of faith. Faith sparks obedience: You 'open the door.' Unfortunately many people's exercise of faith stops there. They have a basic faith in Jesus which evokes obedience to His commands. But there is almost no sense of expectation that the obedience should lead to a further involvement with Jesus, other than that He will be pleased with our obedience. It is like a man who hears a knock, opens the door, smiles and maybe even bows to the one standing on the threshold, then closes the door and waits for the next knock. He may even go around the house on a schedule, opening and closing doors whether anyone is there or not. Many Christians experience their faith as a continual round of opening and closing doors—obedience to the commands of Christ as an end in itself.

Obedience, however, is meant to open us up to a whole new dimension of Christ's working in us. "He gives the Holy Spirit *to those who obey him*" (Acts 5:32). This is the second action of faith. The word of Christ, entering through the doorway of obedience, moves into my life in the power of the Holy Spirit. Now that word is much more than a command. It is a promise. It is Christ himself come to be and do in me all that His Word commands. (See Phil. 2: 12-13.)

When Bob Scott comes to our house things happen that don't happen otherwise. He is a leading layman in our church, but he also happens to be a builder who is the most skilled craftsman I have ever known. Over the years he has kept an eye on our house and taken care of things that needed taking care of.

I remember the Saturday he came to the house with his tool box. "Let's hang a door in the landing so you can have a little privacy in the downstairs room," he said with a chuckle.

When Bob goes to work it is poetry in motion. Not a wasted movement. Every measurement exact. Every action purposeful and precise.

I had complete faith in him. When I saw him drill into the stained paneling in the landing, I knew that he knew what he was doing. When he asked me to give him a hand or fetch him another tool, I did it.

Nordis came home from shopping and called out from the kitchen, "What's all the pounding?" Her voice betrayed a touch of apprehension, recalling the kind of things that sometimes happen when I set out to fix things.

"Bob's here!" I shouted back confidently. "We're hanging a door in the landing."

In an hour the whole job was done, a job I couldn't even have started on my own.

What was my part in the whole operation? Why, I opened the door and let him in! And all the while he was there I expected the door to get hung.

This is the double action of faith that releases the power of love in marriage: Trust swinging open the door of obedience to let Christ in, expectation believing He will work His supernatural love in us by the power of the Holy Spirit.

We need to make clear that our metaphor of a doorway is essentially a picture of spiritual growth. The Lord who has redeemed us 'comes in' to work out His plans for our life. He comes not once, but many times.

It is true, of course, that in one sense Christ is already 'in' every believer. But He does not bring anyone to maturity at a single stroke. He comes to us through His Word in a series of initiatives. Each initiative requires from us a fresh response of obedience, a specific invitation for Him to 'come in.'

It is not unbelievers, but lackadaisical believers, whom Christ speaks to when He says, "Those whom I love, I reprove, and chasten; so be zealous and repent. Behold, I stand at the door and knock; if any one hears my voice and opens the door, I will come in to him and eat with him, and he with me" (Rev. 3:19-20).

Opening a door and inviting in a guest forms one unbroken action. Even as you open the door with one hand, your other hand is already beckoning your guest to enter.

In itself opening a door is a complex feat of coordination. Yet, you don't need to concentrate on it very heavily. With practice it becomes almost an automatic action. What does occupy your thoughts, from the moment you put your hand to the doorknob, is the guest you are about to receive and the purpose of his visit.

In the Christian life, obedience and faith form one unified action. Hebrews 3:19 cites unbelief as the reason for failure in a particular situation. Six verses later the same failure is charged to disobedience.

Much ineffective Christian living, and not least in marriage, can be traced back to an unbiblical separation of faith from obedience. A person may come down heavy on faith. He believes all the right things. He can rattle off doctrines telling who God is, how helpless man is to save himself, what Christ has done, and how wonderfully it's all going to turn out in the end for those who believe. But any further venture of faith involves little more than a restatement, a refining, a more microscopic analysis of one's understanding of God and our relationship with Him.

We cultivate almost to a fault our appreciation of Him who stands on our doorstep. We may indeed strive to obey Him. But our obedience is not mixed with faith. We do not look for anything further from Him than what He has already done in His foundational work of providing for our salvation. We do not expect Him to come into our life and work changes. Once we have believed in Him, any changes that take place depend upon our own efforts. We love Him, we praise Him, we *believe* in Him. But we leave Him standing on the threshold while we go around busily opening and closing doors.

It is faith chopped off at the knees. Faith from a long ago yesterday pointing to a long distant tomorrow, but expecting nothing today. It is faith in Christ without a corresponding faith in the power of the Holy Spirit.

Love's Behavior

It is not enough that faith inspire you to obedience.

The obedience must also trigger a fresh flow of faith. The moment you put your hand to obedience, an expectant faith should begin to rise up in your thoughts.

I think of a young medical student who learned this well.

I hear you, Lord! I'll be there as soon as I can. I saw you heading toward the front entrance. Then you headed around toward that little side door called Take-your-wife-out-for-dessert. She's-hurting-and-needs-to-have-a-good-chance-to-talk.

I'm coming, Lord, I'm coming. Having a little trouble finding time to locate that door. Looks like Tuesday night will be the first chance.

"Table for two, please, How about that little one over in the corner?"

Finally got to the door, Lord. Interesting little door. Funny I never noticed it before, Come in, Lord! My wife has really been depressed the last week or so. Thank you for coming. Things will be different now.

"I think I'm going to have pie with ice cream. How about you? Let's forget the diet for one night."

"Might as well, I guess."

She's really quiet, Lord. Help me say the right thing. I know you're already helping her, deep down.

"Good pie, huh?"

"Uh huh."

"Want to talk about it?"

"About what? The pie?"

"No, about what's bothering you."

No answer. Another bite of pie, slowly.

Operatic pose: "Your problem is my problem!"

Lord, was that too corny?

It's all right, son. She'll open up.

"Well, I guess that's true enough."

"What do you mean?"

"You really want to hear?"

"Try me."

Long pause. "I think I'm pregnant."

"Are—are you sure?"

Son, do you remember the article that just happened to be on the table next to you in the cafeteria last Wednesday?

By that German guy? About our society developing an anti-baby attitude?

The Germans call it Kinderfeindschaft—*looking upon children as enemies.*

"I'm two weeks past my period."

"That means about next . . . February."

Nod. Angry, frustrated: "Five semesters before you graduate."

Son, forget everything else except how she feels right now.

Reaching across the table, taking her hand. "What do you want—a boy or a girl?"

Tears of despair. "We can't afford it! What are we going to do? I'll have to quit work."

"That's okay. We'll work it out."

"I knew you'd say that. But that doesn't solve the problem of getting through Med School. How many times have I heard you say, 'I don't want to end up like my father, quitting school because kids started coming, and plodding along for the next thirty-five years in a job he doesn't like'?"

No answer. Something deep down inside him begins to turn, slowly.

She goes on. "I talked to one of the other girls in the office. Gail Johnson. She works in Purchasing."

Questioning look.

"She's already got two kids, and they don't want any more. She got pregnant last fall and had an abor—"

Reaching across the table and gently laying his finger to her lips. Looking deeply and lovingly into her eyes, slowly shaking his head. "Never in a thousand years."

Tears brim up again, but they are different. They spill in single drops down her cheeks. Tears of release.

Thoughtful, yet quietly commanding: "I learned a new word last week."

Looking at him like a timorous fawn. Only half listening.

"Ran across it in a magazine. It's German: *Kinderfeindschaft.* It means hostility against children. But it's even stronger than that. It means an attitude toward your own children that looks upon them as enemies. This guy said that all the anti-baby emphasis—the pill, abortion, and all—is laying a foundation of *Kinderfeindschaft* in this generation of parents."

"But we want children. It's just that—"

"I know. That's what I said to myself after I read it. We're going to have children; we just want to wait until we get a little better established. But he said something else."

"What was that?"

"*Kinderfeindschaft* begins when a parent chooses his own convenience over the rights and needs of the child. And that can start even before a child is conceived, in the attitude toward pregnancy and parenthood."

"What's the word?"

"*Kinderfeindschaft*—having an attitude toward your kids like they are enemies."

"Do you think people really feel that way about their kids?"

"Maybe not consciously. But he's probably right that our underlying attitudes can be affected by repeated emphasis. The subconscious doesn't pay much attention to all our mental distinctions, like, 'After such-and-such is taken care of, then we want to have a child.' It just picks up impressions. The repeated ritual of contraception—installing a device or swallowing the pill—keeps sending home the message, 'No babies, no babies, no babies.' The subconscious is especially suggestible to symbolic actions involving the body. And our whole society reinforces the same message."

"I never thought about it that way, but I suppose

there could be something to it. You brainwash yourself into thinking that you just can't get pregnant.
So a baby becomes the worst thing that could happen."

*This is a switch, Lord. We were completely locked
in on not having kids before I graduate, but here
we are talking in favor of it. And I'm feeling happy!*

Let her be happy too—happy that she's a woman.

"Want to know what I think?"

"Tell me."

"That you are due for a promotion: From my
Chief Means of Support to . . . Mother." Executive
pose, wagging a silencing finger: "I know, I know.
You haven't had any experience along that line.
But I've been keeping my eye on you, and you are
a real natural for the job. We'll give you a few
months to work into it and we'll make it retroactive
to—when was that? The Saturday afternoon my
biology lab got canceled?"

"That must have been it . . . Daddy."

Daddy! That sounds all right, Lord.

It will take a little getting used to.

I still don't know how it's all going to work out.

*No need to, son. Not now. Tonight you just needed
to share this together as husband and wife, as man
and woman.*

"Sweetheart, thank you for being so sweet last
night."

Holding her. "You know, I feel good this morning.
Like we're more where we ought to be. I think I
was too hung up on being a doctor."

"You're still going to be a doctor!"

"I think so, too. But I'm not so uptight about
it."

"Then you'll be an even better doctor. I've got
to run! I still have a few months on the old job
before I report in as full-time mother. Good-bye!"

*Lord, remember the time you came knocking on
the door called, Bring-your-finances-into-order?*

Yes.

> *It started out with settling up my debts, but it went into my whole attitude toward money. And then that time you knocked on the door, Get-to-know-Scott-Jackson?*
>
> *Yes.*
>
> *Gave me an understanding toward blacks I'd never had before, besides getting to know Scott. And other times, so many of them. And now this— having a baby. I feel like you've done something really big in us.*
>
> *It is big. Basic.*
>
> *Lord, don't ever quit knocking at my door.*
>
> *I don't intend to.*

Of course faith doesn't usually express itself in extended inner dialogue (though it can be helpful from time to time to sharpen our awareness of the Lord's presence). The important thing is: 1) That you recognize the fact that you can *will* to love your wife. You can love her not only when you feel like it. You can love her when your feelings are at low ebb, or even negative. You can love her in obedience to the command of Christ—just as Christ loved us in obedience to the command of the heavenly Father.

2) That with every act of obedience you release a flow of faith. You do not depend upon your own self-motivated love to sustain your wife and your marriage. You look upon that which you do as a way of surrendering yourself to the supernatural love of Christ. What you do (take her out for dessert, remember her birthday, be nice to her brother, talk more, etc.) appears outwardly the same as any other husband doing the same thing. But your inner expectation, and therefore the result, is altogether different. In the midst of this thing that you are doing, the living Christ releases *His* love. And that is what transforms your marriage.

Love's Patience

God wants your human love for one another (often weak and inconstant) to be undergirded by His own divine love. He wants our marriages to find their strength and their stability in Him.

When Steve and Joyce came back to see me, not much seemed to have happened. Steve had made some attempts to extend himself to Joyce, but both of them felt it was awkward. They were disheartened that the old feeling was still absent.

Up to this time I had not put the kind of emphasis on faith such as I have described in the preceding pages. I had simply encountered a number of situations in marriages where a firm decision of the will had reawakened love, sometimes dramatically so.

Remembering their earlier love, I had expected Steve and Joyce to experience the same kind of thing. But as we talked I came to see that this was exactly my mistake: I was looking for Steve to revive his old love for Joyce by a decision of his will. My expectation had focused on him, on his own slumbering resources of love, rather than on the power of Christ's love to come in and transform the whole situation— and this is exactly what I had conveyed to him.

Together with them I had to come at the thing all over again. We couldn't pass lightly over the fact that Steve's love had cooled, as I had done at our first session. We had to accept the situation the way it was. We went further and admitted that there might be nothing that any one of us could do about it.

Then I asked them, "Do you think Christ can do anything about it?"

They didn't know. They guessed maybe He could,

but they didn't seem too sure. At that point neither was I. Faith always trembles when it comes to the brink of that step where everything will depend on God alone.

Yet that is when God can do the most. When we abandon all hope in our own solutions, and surrender to His working in us, He is most free to "give us the Holy Spirit to fill our hearts with his love" (Rom. 5:5, Living Bible).

Steve and I arranged to have lunch together the following day. We talked about him "doing" the same kind of things we had come up with at first. But we came at it differently.

"Nothing important will happen unless Christ comes in and works inside both of you," I said. "It depends on Him."

He sat and didn't say anything.

"Do you think He will?" I asked.

"I don't know."

"Neither do I. If He does, it will make a difference. If not, well . . ." my voice trailed off.

We sat silently for a while.

"Don't you think He will?" he asked at last.

"I don't know. Faith is a funny thing. Sometimes when you think you've got all the faith in the world, everything falls flat. Then you come up against something where you don't have a speck of faith, and things really happen."

"I guess I didn't try very hard."

"I don't think that was the problem. I gave you a bum steer."

"What do you mean?"

"I told you to step out and *do* something. But I didn't say a word to you about faith, about praying for God to intervene in the situation."

He nodded like he understood, but I doubted that he really did.

"I didn't pray either," I continued. "Just expected it to happen automatically, I guess, like I'd seen it happen some other times. We need to pray. Have it out with God. It's the only way anything will happen."

We sat silently for a while, each one thinking his own thoughts. I recalled a verse in the sixth chapter of Hebrews. "Let us leave the elementary doctrines of Christ and go on to maturity . . . and this we will do *if God permits.*" I had told Steve to launch into a program of obedience as though it were a simple human possibility. I had not reckoned on the utter *sovereignty* of God. Even our obedience to His will is by His gracious permission.

Imagine! "Lord, *permit* me to love my wife." Everything, even our obedience, depends upon Him.

"I'm ready to try again if you are," I said.

"What do you mean?"

"I mean that if you will begin to pray for God to do something, I'll pray too. I'll set aside some time every day and lay it out before God—and see if anything happens."

"Okay," he said, with just the slightest hint of resolution. "I really would like to love Joyce again, the way I used to. I really would."

I told him to pray every time he "did" something for his wife—pray for God to use it as an occasion to come in and change things. And not to tell God *how* to change it, just remain open to whatever He would do.

The change was not sudden. And it came about differently than I had looked for. Steve had not been deeply involved in the life of the church. He had started coming when he and Joyce became engaged, and then it was mostly to please her. Prayer was little more than a mealtime formality in his experience.

The first thing that happened was that he began to pray seriously for the first time in his life. It started in regard to the relationship with his wife, but it spread to other things. He began to pray about difficult situations at work, about important decisions that came up, about his own spiritual state.

They attended church regularly. Outwardly they seemed to be a well-adjusted couple. But I knew from our private meetings (mostly with Steve) that they were still a long way from being happy. The going was slow.

Gradually it began to dawn on me what was happening. Jesus was not about to give their marriage a quick shot-in-the-arm to bring back the days of heady passion. As a first order of business He was cementing His relationship with Steve. His concern went beyond the immediate problem. In a patient, unspectacular way He was laying a foundation for the whole future course of their marriage.

I should say, laying *the* foundation for the future course of their marriage. Because what I saw taking place was God moving the marriage off the crumbling foundation of their own feelings for each other and establishing it on Himself.

How many hundred times had I *said* this? "Christ is the foundation of the home. Build your marriage on Christ." But I had been too routine about it. I had taken a couple's relationship with Christ too much for granted.

It takes more than a few sessions of pre-marriage counseling to establish Christ as the foundation of the home where the couple is not already committed to

Him. Even when committed Christians marry, they experience the shaping work of the Holy Spirit in many ways they never did while living singly. They need to be in a situation where their life in Christ can be nurtured, and grow, and become strong.

Several years earlier our church had established the policy that those who wanted to be married in the church must be "active church members," either in our congregation or in some other. I could see the wisdom in that more now than when we first established it. Steve and Joyce had been active in the congregation when they were married. When their marriage ran into difficulty they came seeking help. A groundwork had been laid for the deeper work Christ was now doing in Steve's life.

It was several years before I understood why it all went so slowly. Steve's life in Christ grew steadily. Two more children came along, and he assumed a more active role in their upbringing than the average young husband. He became increasingly considerate of his wife, though I knew she still felt unsure of his love.

One afternoon, at a wedding reception, Joyce was busy serving punch. Steve saw me standing alone to one side for the moment and came over to talk.

"Something in that wedding service struck me today," he said.

"What was that?" I asked.

" 'Cherish.' Just that one word."

"What did it mean to you?"

"Well, that's how I feel about Joyce. I can't exactly explain it. We still have our problems, but when you read that word I had the thought, 'I don't want anything to ever hurt her.' "

I told him that in many people's book that kind

of feeling would be called love.

"I do love her," he said matter-of-factly. "Not like when we were first married, but maybe it's not supposed to be."

"Well, it changes. But don't rule out that it can get even better than when you were first married."

Several months after this Joyce came in to see me. She said things were going much better in their marriage. Steve was more loving than he had been for a long time. "In fact, there isn't a thing I can complain about," she said.

Yet she was disturbed. Disturbed now at her own responses. Just as Steve's love seemed slowly to be returning, her own affections were cooling. The very expressions of love that she had hoped and even cried for, now when they came strangely repelled her.

At this point I was ready to throw up my hands. (Why can't people have nice simple problems to fit our nice simple theories!?)

Steve took it much more calmly when she later shared with him how she felt. He'd been in that place where feeling ebbs away. He *understood*. It seemed actually to release a new flow of love in him.

The Spirit did not repeat in Joyce the slow work He had done in Steve. I don't know whether something akin to a community property law exists in the spiritual realm. But something like that seemed to happen between Steve and Joyce, as I have also seen happen with other couples. It was as though the Spirit opened some inner gate and let flow from Steve to her a practical reliance on Christ which had been building up in him for more than five years.

With him it had been a slow, conscious process. With her it seemed to come spontaneously, and much more quickly. He did not teach her in any formal sense, nor did he lay any demands upon her. He just let the quiet, confident love that the Spirit had worked in him flow to her. And because it *was* a Spirit-wrought love, it touched not only her affections but her spirit as well. Her anxiety and self-condemnation gave place to a growing freedom to love and be loved which she attributed to God.

Several families were on a picnic together a couple of months later, and at lunch I happened to be seated next to Joyce.

"How are things going?" I said, asking the hollow question that probably squelches more genuine conversation than any other phrase in the English language. ("Oh, fine. Just great." How many hurts and yearnings and needs die a quiet, unseen death behind that prepackaged response?)

But she salvaged the conversation by taking my routine words in their literal sense. She leaned toward me and said in a half-whisper, "We've been like on a second honeymoon."

"So . . ." I looked at her quizzically. Her eyes sparkled. I could see that she had been waiting for an opportunity to share this. I nodded, smiling.

Then she made one of those artless passing remarks in which for a moment the shape which has come to a person's soul flashes undistorted into view. "On the first honeymoon we were all alone, just us two. And that's no good. Because God really is a jealous God."

OBEDIENCE IS THE DOOR THAT LETS CHRIST IN

PART THREE

Friends

As the church is subject to Christ, so let wives also be subject in everything to their husbands. Husbands, love your wives, as Christ loved the church and gave himself for her.
—Ephesians 5:24-25

CHAPTER TEN

Different and Equal

"If woman must of necessity be subordinate, she must of necessity be inferior."—Virginia R. Mollenkott

"The headship of the man is not a question of value, dignity or honour, but of order."—Karl Barth

Which one is right? Does headship by its very nature imply superiority, and submission inferiority? Or is headship and submission simply a distinction of functions, two different kinds of responsibility which God has ordered for men and for women?

This is one of the major issues raised by the feminist movement. The way we answer this question will shape our understanding and experience of the husband-wife relationship.

The issue is fogged with misunderstanding because society sees headship in a fundamentally different way than the Bible does. The same words are used but they carry different meanings. The confusion has been compounded because some Christian spokesmen have adopted society's understanding of headship as their point of departure. When this happens the discussion becomes not only confusing, but often simply irrelevant. Terms like "headship" and "submission" may be used, but something different is meant by them than the Bible means.

To handle the question properly, we must specify at the outset which understanding of headship we are

going to talk about. Our concern is to see how headship relates to our life as Christians, specifically in
regard to the marriage relationship. We approach the
question, therefore, from that point of view. What we
say makes sense only in terms of what the Bible says
about headship.

We believe that when that distinction becomes
clear—when you approach headship the way the
Bible does—you will gain a perspective for understanding both the positive and negative features of
the feminist movement, especially as it relates to
marriage. More than that, you will have a grasp
of one of the most important truths about the husband-wife relationship. More than any other single
thing, we have seen a biblical understanding of headship help thousands of couples come into a more
mature and satisfying marriage relationship.

A group of couples who had gone through our
course on family life wrote: "We found that 'Divine
Order' was badly needed in our homes. Although
something was amiss in our families, we just
couldn't put our finger on it. When we began to follow
God's Order, things ran smoother and with less effort. The headship of the husband and the submission
of the wife gives to each a very special and important
role."

The distinctiveness of the biblical concept of headship can be seen most clearly in the way it handles
two specific issues—

1. The status of the wife.
2. The conduct of the husband.

How is a wife regarded who is "subject to her husband"? How does a husband who is "head of the
home" exercise that headship?

The Status of the Wife

"St. Paul, you say that a wife should be subject to her husband. [See Ephesians 5:22.] Doesn't that mean that she is *inferior* to him?"

Some people draw that conclusion from the Apostle's words, for they are convinced no other conclusion is possible. "Subordination by its very nature implies inferiority."

History offers many examples of this kind of thinking. Some theologians of the church have stoutly defended the subordination of women on the ground that women are intrinsically inferior to men. Today feminists just as stoutly oppose the subordination of women on the ground that women are *not* inferior to men. In both cases the understanding of subordination is the same, namely, *subordination implies inferiority.*

Does the Bible teach this? A relationship parallel to the husband-wife relationship is instructive at this point: God the Son (Jesus) is subject to the Father. "The Son can do nothing of his own accord, but only what he sees the Father doing" (John 5:19). This subjection was not limited to His days on earth. It is part of the eternal relationship between the Father and the Son. The active headship of the Father both before and after the incarnation is evident in the opening verses of Hebrews, "God has spoken to us in these last days through a Son, whom *he appointed* the heir of all things, through whom also *he created* the world." I Corinthians 15:28 looks forward to the new age in which all things, including the Son, shall be subject to God the Father. Speaking of the present relationship between Father and Son, the Apostle Paul says, "The head of Christ is God" (1 Cor. 11:3). From eternity to eternity the Son is necessarily subject to the Father.

Yet the Son is not inferior to the Father. Jesus said, "I and the Father are one" (John 10:30). The Sanhedrin condemned Jesus precisely because He claimed equality with God. He did not think it "robbery" to be equal with God (Phil. 2:6). The teaching of the church through the centuries has been that the Son is equal to the Father, "God of God, Light of Light, Very God of Very God."

Subject to God . . . equal to God. That is Christ's relationship to the Father. The subordination carries with it no hint of inferiority.

Status and subordination are two separate issues in Scripture. The Bible does not draw any necessary connection between them. It is possible to be subject to one who is *superior*: Israel was subject to the Lord; believers are subject to Christ; Abraham submitted to the priesthood of Melchizedek, who is described as his superior (Heb. 7:7). Or there can be subordination among *equals*: Christ is equal to God yet subject to God; believers who are equal to one another, "fellow citizens with the saints," are admonished to be "subject to one another" (Eph. 2:19, 5:21). One can even be called to subordinate himself to someone who is *inferior*, as Christ submitted to Pontius Pilate. Status is a sovereign determination of God: We are what God judges us to be. Headship and subordination are sovereign appointments of God: We serve where God calls us to serve. He has put himself under no obligation to link these two things together.

The fact that wives are told to be subject to their husbands tells us nothing about their status. If we had that statement only, we wouldn't know whether they were inferior, equal, or superior to their husbands. We must look further into God's Word to determine what He says about their status.

The Bible makes no distinction between men and women as to status. "In Christ there is neither male nor female" (Gal. 3:28). They are "joint-heirs of the grace of life" (1 Pet. 3:7). They participate in the same baptism.

In regard to the question of status and subordination, the relationship of husband and wife is analagous to that of the Father and the Son. The Apostle Paul draws this parallel in 1 Corinthians 11:3, "The head of every man is Christ, the head of a woman is her husband, and the head of Christ is God."

HEADSHIP: God — Christ* — Man

SUBMISSION: Christ — Man* — Wife

A wife has the same kind of relationship with her husband that Christ has with God: She is equal to her husband; she is subject to her husband. *The stigma of inferiority is as inappropriate to the wife as it is to Christ.* On the other hand, *just as certainly as Christ is subject to God, a wife is subject to her husband.*

The headship of the husband and the submission of the wife is assumed throughout Scripture as the normal and proper order of things. The first chapter of the Bible describes the creation of man(kind) as "male and female," bestowing equal dignity on man and woman (Gen. 1:27). The second chapter, going into greater detail, shows God creating woman to be

---

*It is interesting in this verse to note that both Christ and the husband are *under* headship in one relationship, while they *exercise* headship in the other. The wife experiences the same kind of thing in the "rule of her household" (see 1 Timothy 5:14).

"a helper fit for man." She is brought to the man and he names her, an act expressive of headship. There is no hint that the man, in assuming headship, looks on the woman as inferior. On the contrary, he is delighted with the sense of unity and equality which he has with her, "This at last is bone of my bone and flesh of my flesh" (Gen. 2:23).

In the third chapter we see "the Fall," where the man and the woman disobey God and begin to reap the consequences of their sin. In speaking to the woman, God says, "I will greatly multiply your pain in childbearing; in pain you shall bring forth children, yet your desire shall be for your husband, and he shall rule over you" (Gen. 3:16).

Some have interpreted this to mean that the woman's subjection to her husband came as a result of the Fall, and that in Christ that burden is lifted. But then we should also expect pain in childbirth to be lifted, which is not the case. But even more to the point, the text doesn't yield that meaning when we examine it closely. The burden which God lays upon the woman is increased pain in childbearing. What follows is introduced with the adversative "yet,"* indicating not an additional burden, but something contrasting with the burden. Two things are mentioned: 1) Your desire shall be for your husband; 2) He shall rule over you. If one argues that in Christ the husband's rule is lifted, then according to logic a woman's sexual desire in marriage should also be set aside. No one seems to be making that case.

A more natural interpretation is that God, along with the punishment, speaks a word of mercy and

---

*The Hebrew *w'al* is correctly translated in the RSV as the adverbial adversative "yet," not as "and" (KJV).

encouragement, something He often does when pronouncing judgment. The relationship with her husband which existed before the Fall will carry over and be a comfort and strength to her, the relationship being described in terms of its two essential characteristics, sexual union and headship.

Some dismiss the man's headship in marriage as a purely cultural phenomenon. The New Testament writers, they say, simply reflect the customs of their own age and culture. When we examine the matter more closely, however, the case is not that simple.

Does the picture of marriage which the Apostle Paul depicts in Ephesians 5:22-23 reflect the general culture in which it was written? In order to answer this, we must consider briefly the role of women in that time.

In Greek culture women were generally considered inferior to men, and were kept in seclusion in the family. Macedonia and Asia Minor were exceptions to this general pattern.* In Roman culture women enjoyed greater practical, if not legal, freedom than in Greek culture; women participated more freely in religious activities, and this aided in the spread of Christianity.

In Macedonia, after the time of Alexander the Great, women began to have a relatively greater measure of freedom. This was due largely to the fact that Macedonian dynasties produced an extraordinary succession of able and masterful women such as Arisonoe, Berenice, and Cleopatra. These women played a large part in civic affairs, they received envoys, built temples, founded cities, engaged mercen-

---

*Thomas Kraabel, Chairman of Religious Studies, University of Minnesota. "Status of Women in Asia Minor," unpublished monograph.

aries, commanded armies, held fortresses, and acted on occasion as regents or co-rulers.

In Asia Minor (the western part of modern Turkey, where Ephesus and Colossae were located), women enjoyed unusual privileges and status. A practical equality between the sexes had emerged in considerable measure before the Christian era. This was especially evident in the area of religion. The most striking feature in the native religion and society of Asia Minor is the important part played by women.

In Jewish culture the position of women is somewhat paradoxical. On the one hand, there is the well-known saying of the synagogue service, "Blessed art thou, O Lord our God, King of the universe, who hast not made me . . . a woman." On the other hand, there are the lofty words concerning womanhood in Proverbs 31. The paradox makes sense only if we recognize the high value which Jewish culture placed upon woman in her proper sphere of service, which was the home. Legally she had few rights, but in the home she held a place of unparalleled dignity. The "emancipation" movement in Asia Minor appeared to have had some effect on Jewish culture. According to one inscription there appears to have been even a ruler of a synagogue who was a woman. On the whole, however, the Jewish culture would be in accord with the form of family life outlined in Paul's writings, and could be seen as a source for it.

Some New Testament passages seem to reflect a social setting like that in Asia Minor, or an attitude toward women which would accord with that kind of society. Jesus conversed publicly with the Samaritan woman, a break with Jewish custom (John 4:7ff.). Women had a prominent place in the company of those who followed Jesus. Some of them were of independent means, and contributed to the support of the apostolic company (Luke 8:2-3). Women such as Lydia appear to have had a relatively independent economic status (Acts 16:14).

The New Testament letters in which the headship of the husband is set forth (Ephesians and Colossians) were written to churches in Asia Minor, where we find evidence of a "women's emancipation movement." In this setting the New Testament teaching concerning men-women roles would be at some variance with the prevailing culture, a corrective rather than an accommodation.*

This is further reflected in the context of the scriptures themselves. Ephesians 5:22-33 is set in a larger section (4:17-6:9) dealing substantially with practices which the Apostle wants to correct. The context would suggest that he is advocating a structure of family life which was not generally being followed, or at the least was in danger of being eroded away. It would seem that he saw the women's emancipation movement carrying things to extremes, and therefore introduced a word of correction.

Further, the New Testament presents its case on the basis of "first principles" or "orders of creation." So far as its own self-understanding goes, it does not understand the man-woman relationship primarily as a cultural phenomenon, but as belonging to the order of nature (1 Cor. 11:3, 14; 1 Tim. 2:13-14). The image for marriage in Ephesians, that of the church as the

---

*An interesting sidelight is provided in connection with the apocryphal book, *Acta Pauli.* The author, according to Tertullian, confessed that he had committed his forgery for "love of Paul." By this he meant that he was trying to present Paul more favorably to the Christian women of Asia Minor than the Pastoral Letters had done. It is in works like this, rather than in canonical scripture, that we see an attempt to accommodate to the prevailing culture.

Bride of Christ, transcends culture. The biblical pattern may certainly be understood as having a validity which goes beyond culture.

In Ephesians the Apostle addresses words not only to husbands and wives but also to slaves, and this has raised questions for some. They recognize that St. Paul says, "Wives, be subject to your husbands." But, they say, he also says, "Slaves, be obedient to your masters." Therefore, they conclude, to say that 20th-century women should continue to be subject to their husbands is as foolish as to make a case for the continuance of slavery.

This kind of reasoning, however, misses Paul's point. In these verses the Apostle is not discussing the relative merits of slavery and freedom; as, indeed, he is not discussing the relative merits of marriage as over against celibacy. (He discusses both of these questions in other places.) In Ephesians, he is telling people who *are* married, or who *are* slaves, how they should conduct themselves. If we say, "We do not believe in slavery today," the parallel is not "We do not believe in the husband's headship." The parallel is, "We do not believe in marriage." To draw a comparison between slavery and marriage in this context does not make a case against headship in marriage, but against marriage itself.

The Bible makes no case for slavery as a divine institution. In 1 Corinthians 7:21 Paul says, "If you can gain your freedom, avail yourself of the opportunity." Marriage is treated in an altogether different way. It *is* divinely instituted. It is created and structured by God. The relationship of husband and wife is modeled upon the relationship of Christ and the church. Nothing could make the case for headship more clear: "As the church is subject to Christ, so let wives also be subject in everything to their husbands" (Eph. 5:24). As little as the church can set aside the headship of Christ, can we set aside the headship of the husband. It is not a mere cultural phenomenon. It has its model and source in an eternal reality, the love of Christ for His Bride, the church.

Neither the argument that submission implies inferiority nor the argument that headship is only a cultural phenomenon stands up under scrutiny. The Bible, without contradiction, sees the wife as fully equal to her husband, and as fully subject to him.

The Conduct of the Husband

A middle-aged wife, tears brimming in her eyes, says, "He just completely dominates me. I feel like a nothing. How long am I supposed to take it? After all, I'm a person too."

A wife in her early 30's writes, "I agree with the principle of 'headship.' It gives a definite sense of identity, and a proud position in the home. (This is very important in today's society.)"

It is in the midst of these real-life situations—in the midst of heartaches and joys—that we have sought to help people enter into God's order for their marriages. We know that it doesn't happen easily. It may involve real struggle and suffering, especially where one of the partners is indifferent. We nevertheless believe that God does have an order for marriage, and that the headship of the husband and the submission of the wife is central to that order. Indeed, as Steve Clark points out in his excellent book, *Man and Woman in Christ,** "Care and subordination are

---

*Stephen Clark (South Bend, Ind.: Servant Books, 1978).

the key elements which the New Testament stresses. Someone who presents the New Testament teaching on husbands and wives and leaves out husband-wife care and subordination has neglected the one point that the New Testament has explicitly enjoined."

The problem is not with God's order, but with husbands and wives who do not understand and practice it. As G. K. Chesterton once said, "It is not that Christianity has been tried and found wanting; it has been found difficult and left untried."

If God's order is going to work, husbands must get a grip on how a Christian man exercises authority, and wives on how a Christian woman submits to that authority. Jesus said, "You know that those who are supposed to rule over the Gentiles lord it over them, and their great men exercise authority over them. But it shall not be so among you; but whoever would be great among you must be your servant, and whoever would be first among you must be slave of all" (Mark 10:42-44).

Headship is a means of *serving* others. That is its essential function. One who exercises headship must understand it first of all as a position from which to serve.

This does not mean that one in headship is under the authority of those he serves and takes orders from them. On the contrary, the particular kind of service he gives them is the *service of leadership.*

As head, a husband serves his family by giving them intelligent, sensitive leadership. His headship is not meant for domineering and stifling his wife and children, but for leading, protecting, providing, and caring for them.

* * *

Jerry and Priscilla Wellon got jolted out of twelve years of rudderless marriage when Priscilla reported that they couldn't get any more baby sitters to take care of their four children.

"What do you mean, 'We can't get any more baby sitters'?" Jerry asked, not bothering to glance up from his boating magazine.

"I mean the word's gotten around," Priscilla said, snatching the magazine out of his hands. "Our kids are monsters and nobody wants to take care of them. You know what they did to Angie Peterson when I left them with her last Saturday? They lured her out into the backyard and then turned the hose on her."

"They did?"

"Yes, 'they did,' " she said, mimicking him, barely able to control her agitation.

"Well, why didn't you—why didn't you say something about it?"

"So you could yell at them for five minutes, and then forget about the whole thing the way you always do? Jerry, you've got to *do* something about them. I'm ready for the booby hatch."

That incident was fresh in his mind, Jerry said, when he saw an article in the local paper announcing a seminar on family life at our church, with special emphasis on raising children. They were not church-going people, but they were frustrated enough to give it a try.

For the first time in his life Jerry heard about headship. "I didn't even know what the word meant," he recounted later. "Frankly, I expected to hear a lot of platitudes about praying and going to church, and being thoughtful and loving. Instead, I got a whole new concept of order and responsibility.

"This thing of being 'head' really got to me. Priscilla's no women's libber. She's always let me be the boss. The thing of it was, I wasn't doing it. As long as the roof didn't fall in, I just let things slide. The kids could be having a pitched battle in the living room, and I'd just go on reading, or go out and work on my boat."

The seminar went on for seven weeks. They didn't miss a single session, but they had to alternate weeks, because they couldn't get a baby sitter. One week Jerry came, the next week Priscilla.

The fifth session dealt with "The Priesthood of Parents," and Jerry was attending. Afterward he came up and talked with me.

"You know, this is all really new to us," he said. "We've never gone to church. How can a guy be a 'spiritual head' when he doesn't know one end of the Bible from the other?"

It was interesting to talk with him. Sometimes church people have taken biblical truth in little doses for so long that they build up an immunity to it. Jerry made no bones about his ignorance of spiritual truth, but he was refreshingly open to it. I suggested some things they might read together, to get family worship started.

Later, when I visited them in their home, they shared with me some of the changes that had begun to take place in their family.

"After that third seminar—the one on disciplining children—our kids had one rude awakening," Priscilla said with a kind of grim satisfaction.

"But the relationships have improved a thousand percent," Jerry interposed.

"They really have," Priscilla agreed. "Tell him about Ginger, Jerry."

Ginger was their nine-year-old. She had been particularly difficult to deal with for something over a year. They had attempted every way they knew of trying to control her, but nothing worked.

"When you mentioned this thing about spanking, we didn't know what to think. We've never spanked our kids. But nothing else had worked, so we decided to give it a try."

"We sat down and explained it to them first," Priscilla put in.

"Yes, we told them that we hadn't been doing right as their parents, and that from now on we were going to do it the way the Bible says. We'd tell them what we expected of them, and if they disobeyed or were rebellious, there'd be a spanking.

"Well, with Ginger it went in one ear and out the other. We'd tried forty-nine different approaches, and this was just number fifty."

"Until Jerry told her to help her sister Rita wash up the supper dishes," Priscilla said.

"That's right. I told her to do it, and when the job was half done she took off down the street to play with a friend. I brought her back, took her into her room, and gave her a spanking."

Priscilla's eyes positively sparkled as she recalled the incident. "Pastor, you won't believe it, but we've had more love between us and Ginger in the last six days than we had in the last six months. I can't believe it. She's a different girl."

Another thing Jerry tried was taking the children out to dinner, just to get a chance to talk with them. "This fellow you quoted said to take them out one at a time," he said, "but with four of them that's a little tough. I've taken them by two's. They really like it."

Their own relationship went through some changes too. "We were operating pretty much independently of one another," Jerry said. "She'd make her decisions and I'd make mine, and as long as we didn't get in each other's backyard things would chug along fairly well. But then we'd both jump in on the same thing, and that's when there'd be fireworks. Now we talk things over a lot more."

"I never realized how many things I had just taken over," Priscilla said. "This being submissive takes some getting used to. But I really like it when we check things out with each other."

One thing that helped them enormously was their willingness to make changes gradually. Sometimes when people first encounter teaching on family order —and it seems to be especially true of young husbands—they take the bit in their teeth and try to "take charge" all in one jump. The result is too many, too sudden changes, ill-considered decisions from which one has to retreat, mounting resentments and misunderstanding, and often a lapsing back into old ways. When you supplant old ways more gradually, the new way of doing things has a better chance to take root.

Initially Jerry and Priscilla concentrated on training their children. But they soon discovered that this required them to re-evaluate their own lives. What kind of example were they living out before the children? Jerry began to see things in himself and in Priscilla that needed to change.

"He really did a number on my laziness," Priscilla said. "That's about the only real fight we got into. But it was worth it, because I had really always felt guilty about my sloppy housekeeping."

Little by little the drift and irresolution in their

marriage began to give way to stability and direction. The whole family began to come to church. Nobody remarked anything special about their children. Once it was clearly communicated to them, and the parents followed through, they adjusted rather quickly to a new standard of discipline. We have seen this happen as a fairly normal thing, especially when the children are still under twelve years of age. Children thrive where an atmosphere of love is structured with order and routine.

Several months later, following an evening service, both Jerry and Priscilla stayed at the altar for some time. I had been talking to people at the door of the church and was ready to lock up when I saw them kneeling there. I sat down in one of the pews, not wanting to disturb them. After a while Jerry looked around and saw that everyone else had left. He nudged Priscilla and they got up. They spotted me as they stepped down from the altar area.

"Sorry, Pastor," Jerry said. "We just wanted to pray."

"No problem with that. Can I be of any help?"

As they came up to me I saw that Priscilla had been crying. "Is anything wrong?" I asked.

She shook her head, smiling, and wiped away the tears with the back of her hand. "Last night, after the kids were in bed, we got to talking about all the things that have been happening to us. And the next thing we knew we were both on our knees, praying and asking Christ to come into our hearts."

"It was really different," Jerry said.

"I was bawling and he just kept saying, 'It's okay, honey, it's okay.' It's just that I've never been happy like that in my life."

"Tonight we felt like we wanted to sort of—" Jerry fumbled for the right word.

"You mean you wanted to 'seal' it, or 'confirm' it in some way?" I asked.

"That's right. You know, Pastor, I've never even been baptized. You've got a real raw recruit on your hands."

Jerry and Priscilla entered into family order the way most people in our acquaintance have, experimentally. They began to put the biblical teaching to the test of practical experience. They found out that it works. They discovered that the headship of the husband and the submission of the wife is not an exalting of one and a degrading of the other. It is the finest way that two different and equal people can live and grow together in the most intimate of human relationships.

WE ARE WHAT GOD SAYS WE ARE, EQUAL

WE SERVE WHERE GOD CALLS EACH TO SERVE...

In Headship
In Submission

CHAPTER ELEVEN

The Joy of Submission

What does it mean to be a "submissive wife"? Is that word applicable to 20th-century life? Many voices today say No.

Western culture has looked to psychology and the social sciences for guidance and direction in our social relationships. We seem to have implicit faith in their prescriptions. It's time we ask, "What results have these prescriptions brought? Do they warrant the kind of faith we have put in them?" Our own study of family life, begun in 1963, was prompted by the sad state of a number of families, including our own, that had been trying the prescriptions offered by our culture.

One thing we came to realize was simply this: the basic orientation of our culture is away from God. Its prescriptions for family life do not take God into account.

Submission—God's Prescription

Psalm 1:1 says, "Blessed is the man who walks not in the counsel of the ungodly." Perhaps the blessedness of family life has been lost because we have too often walked in the counsel of the ungodly, sources that do not recognize God.

We have found that God's prescription for family life works well even though it runs contrary to some modern trends. When we measure other theories against God's Word, we can sort out those that are helpful. But those which appeal only to our ego or selfishness we can discard.

Some people who say that biblical principles of family life can't possibly work have an inadequate view of biblical principles. The old, severe, sometimes cruel, Prussian authoritarianism is not an example of God's order for the family. 1 Peter 3:8, immediately after it has admonished both husband and wife, says, "Finally all of you should be of one and the same mind, united in spirit, sympathizing with one another, loving each other, compassionate and courteous, tenderhearted and humbleminded." That doesn't describe cruel authoritarianism.

God's order for the family is not a legalism, or one member picking out a verse to impose on another family member. It is a life of faith, a life in which we accept the trustworthiness of God and the guidance in the Bible, a life that depends on His life-changing grace in everyday situations. It is a Spirit-wrought harmony in our family relationships. It is the creative effect of the Holy Spirit working God's order in us in our daily lives.

It is mainly for order in the relationships of the home that the woman is given the role of being submissive to her husband. In this day of rebellion the idea of order is suspect. We are tempted by the idea that if we could get rid of all forms of order we could escape suffering. Perhaps this delusion was believable fifteen or twenty years ago, but in the meantime we have seen that lawlessness results in greater suffering. Order is important to us as human beings. When we live in chaos we experience senseless suffering. We tear ourselves to pieces like two gears that don't mesh. We need order. God knows that. God is a good God. His order is good.

Submission and Honor

What is submission? Does it mean being a door-mat, a colorless dish rag?

Does it mean never having a strong opinion and saying so?

Allegre Harrah says, "If your husband walks all over you, you are lying down on the job." God knows what He has created in women. He has our full potential in mind when He says, "Wives, be subject to your husbands."

God wants each woman to be a genuine person. He works with each one in terms of her own personality and her own everyday relationships to make her the genuine, submissive person He intends her to be. He doesn't expect her to adopt some pious facade in order to be more acceptable to Him.

On the other hand, in a culture where women are culturally inculcated to be aggressive and demanding it is not irrelevant to ask, "Am I out of order? Am I so demanding that my husband abdicates headship in order to have peace?"

God's order does not demean a woman. What God has in mind for us as Christian wives is not beneath us.

It is a place of honor.

It is a place of power.

It is a place of peace.

It is a place of satisfaction.

It is a place of heart rest.

It is a desirable place.

A matron in our congregation to whom many women look for wisdom and insight said, "The position that God has given our husbands is not for degrading the wife, but for her well-being. We should feel cherished by God that He has arranged things this way."

God's order is an expression of His wisdom and love. If He says, "Be submissive," there is nothing better.

Submission and Disagreement

What is submission? Practically speaking, it means recognizing that the husband has the responsibility for making the final decision when you don't agree.

It isn't bad to disagree. Someone has said, "If you always agree one of you is unnecessary." We have come to see the truth in that, but when we were first married we were threatened by disagreements. We have come to see that the differences between husband and wife are part of God's order and that includes differences of opinion, disagreements.

"The task we face is to say Yes without reserve to being different, for only then can we complete each other, give to each other, and become truly one with each other." [1]

Dr. Hans Selye, an expert on coping with stress, says that stress for one person isn't stress for another person. If you make a turtle run as fast as a race horse, you will kill him. If you hold a race horse down to a turtle pace, you will kill him. [2]

In marriage we sometimes conclude, "I'm a turtle. What am I doing hooked up with this race horse?"

God, however, knows that if He puts two turtles together they will never get the kids off to school on time. If He puts two race horses together, they will burn out in six months. So He uses the race horse to spur on the turtle and the turtle to slow down the race horse. Sometimes it causes stress but we need our mate to complement and stretch our own personality.

We can accept that it isn't bad to disagree. But it is bad to make a full scale war out of every disagreement. We need to know how to deal with disagreements. We need to consider our spouse's point of view, learn how to make agreements, and then live by those agreements.

This is one agreement we came to in a situation of conflict. Our house is a block from the church and most of the time Larry walks home for lunch. I would begin expecting him about 12:00, but if he had something on his desk that he wanted to finish, he wouldn't come until it was done. Or the phone might ring just as he was leaving the office and he would be held up by a long conversation, unable to call me. Or someone would catch him with a question or problem along the way.

I felt like I was in limbo until he came. I kept looking out the window. I hated to start in on any new project. It irritated me—perhaps beyond its real importance, but often it is the little irritations that wear us down and cause problems. It was so little that we never took the time and brain power to work out an agreement that would solve the problem.

One day I happened into Larry's office a little before noon. A priest from a local Catholic parish was standing there talking to him. The three of us visited for a few minutes. When the priest glanced at his watch and saw that it was five minutes to twelve, he said, "Oh, I have to get home for lunch," and hurriedly excused himself.

Well, that did it! "If you have a housekeeper,

you have to be on time," I thought to myself, "but you can keep a wife waiting half the afternoon."

We decided it was time to make an agreement. Twelve-thirty would be "eating together time." If either one of us couldn't or didn't want to be there at twelve-thirty, it wasn't necessary to notify the other, but the one coming late would not have company for lunch. The one who was there would be free to eat without waiting. It was a simple solution and satisfied both of us.

Another way to deal with disagreement is to postpone the decision. Many decisions don't have to be made immediately. Husband and wife can compare points of view and ask the Holy Spirit to bring them to unity.

But if the time comes that a decision must be made, and there is not agreement, then the husband must make the decision. That is the responsibility which goes with headship. Anyone who thinks that having the responsibility is easier and more pleasant than submitting probably hasn't had the responsibility.

My problem isn't that I want the responsibility. I just want to muddy up the decision-making process by having my own way. This introduces competition and vying for authority in the marriage.

One marriage counselor told a troubled couple, "It doesn't matter what it is that starts the fight— in-laws, money, children, vacation—what you are really fighting about is, 'Who will be the boss?' "

Competition and rebellion are not components of a truly loving relationship. Yet competition is a component of many marriages today where perhaps love does not reign in all areas. Clearing out the competition by establishing well-understood roles in the decision-making process creates an atmosphere where love can grow.

Some protest the idea of a role. But everyone fulfills a role of one kind or another. A role can be a healthy, helpful thing. It should be a guiding principle, not a straitjacket.

The radical feminists downgrade and belittle the role of homemaker and mother, yet they are seeking with all the power of the modern media to impose another role upon women. When the verbal smoke clears, what you are left with is the idea that the only life worth living is a man's life. The attributes of a man, the accomplishments of a man, the goals of a man—these are the things worth doing or striving for.

Or, if it is not entirely the drive to be masculine, it tends toward unisex. "Women are in danger of extinction in the drive to be neuter." [3]

Our society needs women and what they can contribute in their role as homemakers. A woman is the natural person to make family survival and development a career.[4] In the perspective of a whole lifetime, I believe there is no more rewarding, fulfilling career than that of wife, mother, and homemaker. To have your husband say, "Many women have done excellently, but you surpass them all . . . ," to have your children rise up and call you blessed (Prov. 31:29, 28), that is a reward and fulfillment beyond anything the academic or business world can provide.

Frustration and failure have discouraged many women, causing them to consider other fields of accomplishment. It doesn't have to be. We can learn to be effective in our family relationships. Deep down we know that is our greatest opportunity, our first duty. With God's order it can also be our greatest joy.

Yes, headship and submission are roles. Yet there is room for infinte variety because of temperament, abilities, likes, and dislikes. The couple that follows God's order for headship and submission find that it facilitates peace and order in the home. It allows God to help them become a wife or a husband in the most creative and fulfilling way possible. It builds their friendship.

Competition is not a right relationship between men and women. It damages something precious and basic in both. Men draw back from competing with women, or else begin to treat them as if they were men. Women seem often to become hard in competing with men.

Since I stopped competing and admitted that I don't have all the good ideas in the world, I have been amazed (horrified) at the number of times Larry is right—when I was solidly convinced beforehand that I was right. When I gave up competing, I came to appreciate the good judgment and protection of my husband.

Another thing I discovered: When he doesn't have to vie for authority he hears better. He is more open to my ideas. We come more readily to agreement and consensus.

Submission and Joy

Submission is not something we work in ourselves. It is something Christ works in us. My prayer is not, "I'm going to be a submissive wife." But rather, "Lord, make me a submissive wife. Give me your submissive spirit. Show me what it means for my personality, my situation."

If Larry and I don't agree, I "submit" my plan, my ideas, my insight, my objections, my fears. (I have learned not to submit my anger. It used to be that I was so convinced of being right that it made me angry when Larry disagreed. I Corinthians 13 taught me that I can be as right as right can be, but if I do not have love I will accomplish nothing. If I don't have the love to discuss something in a kind and informative tone of voice, no matter how right I am, I'm wrong!) Then I pray, "Lord, if you think I have a good idea, you convince him." That can be trusted to the Lord.

Sometimes He does change my husband's mind. If my plan loses, however, I still have joy. The joy of submission is one of God's surprises because it is altogether unexpected, coming at a time when my will has been thwarted. It is a confirming sign that this is God's order. The whole experience gives a sense of well-being that those with the upraised, clenched fist will never know.

Submission is not a harsh order. It is a humanizing, love-producing role which leaves room for individual differences and mutuality.

It takes faith to believe in God's order. But that is exactly what He calls us to—a life of trust in His goodness, a life where His grace and His heart-changing power is available to us. He assures us that He has "plans for us, plans for good and not for evil, to give us a future and a hope" (Jer. 29:11). God's order of headship and submission helps us enter into that plan and that future.

THE JOY
OF SUBMISSION
IS
ONE
OF GOD'S
SURPRISES

CHAPTER TWELVE

The First Word

What kind of word-association would most people come up with for "headship"? A lop-sided majority would probably land on a word like "authority," or something close to it. But "authority" is not the first word for headship. The first word is submission.

A man first begins to understand his calling as 'head' when he recognizes that he himself is under headship. He is responsible to someone higher than himself. "The head of every man is Christ" (1 Cor. 11:3). In order to be fully effective as head of his wife and family, a man must submit to the headship of Christ. Proper headship operates within a clearly defined chain-of-responsibility. If the chain is broken at any link, authority becomes impaired.

A Roman centurion once came to Jesus and asked Him to heal his servant. He believed Jesus could do this, and his belief was rooted in a penetrating grasp of the nature of authority.

"I am a man under authority," he said, "with soldiers under me. I say to one 'Go,' and he goes; and to another, 'Come,' and he comes" (Matt. 8:9).

We might have expected him to say, "I am a man who *has* authority . . . " But the centurion was much humbler and wiser. He recognized that his authority to command a soldier rested upon the fact that he, as a Roman officer, stood properly lined up in a chain-of-command. His word, finally, was backed up by the emperor himself.

The centurion recognized in Jesus a similar authority in the spiritual realm. The fact that Jesus could command spiritual forces rested upon the fact that He, too, was "under authority," that He was properly lined up in *God's* chain-of-command.

Christ's authority is rooted in His submission to God. A husband's authority grows out of his submission to Christ. He orders the life of the family not on his own authority; he does it as one living under the headship of Christ. He exercises authority over his wife and children as the personal representative of Christ. In setting a course for his family, he does not follow his own preferences; he follows the word of his Lord.

Paradoxically, therefore, the man who wants to be a successful husband does not focus first of all upon his wife and children, but upon Christ. If he loses his personal standing under Christ, he loses his footing as a husband. He may be concerned. He may expend great effort at being a model husband. But if he is not living in submission to Christ's authority, he is building on sand. A wife has no firm ground for submitting to her husband's authority if he himself is not under authority.

Submission to authority is always tested at the point where you do not want to obey. It is no test of submission to go along with your head when you agree with him. That only makes sense. But when he asks you to do something you don't want to do, then you find out whether you are truly submissive, or whether you only have a relationship of convenience.

* * *

Gary Espinosa was affectionately referred to as the "Macaroni Maharaja" by his friends. He had inherited a small macaroni factory from his father, and built it into a prosperous business.

He was a man of strong, outspoken opinions, and proud of it. "You don't have to wonder what I think about something," he would say, "I'll tell you." And he did, in no uncertain terms.

He was a likable person, outgoing, and generous to a fault. But whenever a difference of opinion surfaced in his general vicinity, fire would come into his eye. His jaw would go taut, and his voice would come out in staccato machine gun bursts. The setting was immaterial: It could be his family, the Rotary Club, the office, a dinner party, a PTA meeting, a political caucus. When Gary had an opinion he stated it in the strongest, most abrasive terms possible.

Sometimes people became angry with him, but most often, especially in his family and at the office, they just let the matter drop. They might not agree with him but disagreeing wasn't worth the effort. People found ways to get around him without provoking a confrontation.

When he was in his mid-30's he had a powerful religious awakening. Though he came from a nominally Catholic family, his wife was Protestant, and after his awakening he joined his wife's church. Before long he was deeply involved in the life of the congregation, regularly studying the Bible, and serving on several committees.

It was on one of these committees that God began to deal with him about his opinions. Serving on the committee with him was Al Gallagher, a Junior High science teacher. He had been a state champion de-

bater in college, and he enjoyed a good discussion.
But he was essentially an easy-going person. He did
not become emotionally involved in controversy. He
weighed different points of view with remarkable
objectivity, and assumed, almost naively, that others
did the same.

He and Gary had served on the committee together for about two months when their first difference
of opinion arose. Gary launched in with his usual
abandon. When he had finished Al said, "Well, that
is an interesting point-of-view. Mine is a little different . . . " He was not threatened by Gary, nor by the
difference that had arisen between them. He didn't
get angry, nor did he quietly acquiesce, the two reac-
tions Gary was most accustomed to. He probed the
issue with questions and observations that Gary
hadn't thought of. In the end the committee decided
to go along with what Al proposed.

Gary left the meeting seething with frustration.
By morning he had slept it off; he was not a person
to carry around aggravation. But he gave no thought
to changing his ways.

When the next confrontation came up, Gary was
no better prepared for it than he had been the first
time. He sounded off at length without restraint.
Then, one by one, Al's quiet probing set his argu-
ments aside.

This went on for some months and neither man
made much of it. They actually became quite close
friends, though they seemed to have a knack for wind-
ing up on opposite sides of almost any question that
came up.

It first dawned on Gary that something needed to
change when a woman on the committee said to him,

"You always sound so angry when you disagree with anyone."

"I believe in stating my opinions," he said categorically.

"Well, you could do it more pleasantly," she said icily, and turned away to speak to another woman.

Gary mulled over that little exchange for the next two weeks. Was he too blunt in the way he disagreed with people? He began to experience what many people testify to when God begins to deal with something in their life, a "piling up" of evidences. In his daily Bible reading he had three days on 1 Corinthians 13:4-7, "Love is patient and kind; love is not jealous or boastful; it is not arrogant or rude. Love does not insist on its own way; it is not irritable or resentful; it does not rejoice at wrong, but rejoices in the right. Love bears all things, believes all things, hopes all things, endures all things."

The minister preached a sermon in which he said, "The cross of Christ must deal with . . . our ingrained habits . . . and settled opinions . . . " That was the only sentence he remembered, but it was enough.

An advertising brochure came across his desk at work, with a lead line in big red letters, *"Do people take your opinion seriously?"* He had always thought so. Now he was not so sure. Maybe his "coming on strong" didn't convince people so much as it just turned them off.

The *coup de grace* came when he and his wife were getting ready to go to open house at the school where their two children were enrolled. Ten-year-old Janet said, "Daddy, Mrs. Peck is a really neat teacher and I like her a lot, so don't tell her what you don't agree with, huh?"

The next time the committee met at church, Gary

asked Al Gallagher to go out for a cup of coffee afterwards. Without any embellishment he told Al what was bothering him.

"I think the Lord is saying something about the way I come on with my opinions. Too strong."

Al nodded. "You come on strong, all right."

"Does it bother you?"

"Not particularly."

"That's what I thought. You and I disagree, but we still get along."

"People are different. I notice that they back off from you when you start to argue. They're afraid of you."

"They're not afraid of you."

Al shrugged.

"I guess I just have a hard time keeping my opinion to myself when I feel strongly about it," Gary said.

Al pursed his lips. "Maybe you need to do with your opinions what I had to do with my golf."

"What was that?"

"I was quite a golfer. At one time I even considered going pro. But it got to be too big a thing. I was going off Saturdays and Sundays, leaving the wife and kids alone.

"The Lord began to get to me on it. I was going golfing whenever *I* wanted to, not when *He* wanted me to."

"Did you give it up?"

"For a while I thought it might come to that. I quit altogether for about six months. Then I felt free to come back to it. I go out a couple times a month now."

"I guess it never even entered my head to ask whether the *Lord* wants me to spout my opinion."

"I'm glad you had the nerve to bring this up, Gary. I think it *is* the Lord talking to you. The way you come on sometimes, it antagonizes people."

"That's the picture I've been getting."

"If what you have to say is from the Lord, you don't have to push it. Here's the way I'd go at it. Before you offer your opinion, shoot off a prayer. Ask whether you should speak. And *how* you should speak. That's probably even more important."

"Look, Al, if I sound off when you're around—you know, in the wrong way—give me a high sign or something. I really want to deal with this thing."

"Okay."

"I probably do it more than I realize. At home and the office, too." He laughed disparagingly. "I don't know who'll nail me there."

Al pointed his thumb upward, and grinned. "*He'll* take care of that. Basically it's not the talking anyway. That's one of the things I learned with the golf."

"What do you mean?"

"The thing He's really after is *us*. He wants to know if He really is Lord in our lives. The golf or the talking are tests to see how real and practical our submission to Him is."

"Man, you're farther down the road than I am. You should have been a preacher."

"I was."

"You were?" Gary registered surprise.

Al nodded. "For seven years."

"What happened?"

"Too much pressure. Too many people expecting you to do too many things. I just wasn't cut out for it. So I went back and got my teaching credential."

Gary nodded. Not because he understood, but because he did not want to intrude further on the other man's privacy.

A little later, when he was driving home alone, Gary thought to himself, "Something really happened tonight. I can feel it."

What happened to Gary was exactly what Al Gallagher had told him would happen: Christ came in and took over a particular area of his life. Over a period of time he learned to submit his strongly voiced opinions to Christ. The Spirit worked in him a new gentleness, and a responsiveness to other people's opinions.

Several years later, at a men's retreat, Gary shared how this change had affected things in his family and his business. "I used to think that being 'boss' meant being right all the time, and having things go my way."

He shared a number of examples, some of them hilarious, of how his family and his employees had learned to wangle their own way by contriving situations that would provoke him into stating a strong opinion in support of what they wanted to do.

"What I—or they—want to do is not the important thing." Gary said, "It's what *God* wants to do that counts. And what I've discovered in my own family and in my business is this: When I'm trying to obey Christ, they quit trying to get around me. The whole relationship is more relaxed and open, and honest."

* * *

A husband's obedience to Christ must get down to everyday realities. It must touch on the areas of his life where he doesn't *want* to obey. It must involve a real surrender of his will. His headship in the family will only be as authentic as his submission to Christ is authentic.

How his wife responds to his headship is less his concern than it is Christ's. If things do not go well between him and his wife, if she is restive under his authority, the first thing a man needs to do is pray—

"Lord, you see how it is between us. What's the matter? Why aren't you able to channel your authority through me? Am I wrong? Is she? What do *you* want to do about it?"

Dale Givens prayed just that kind of a prayer one evening. He had spoken a sharp word to his wife about her habit of always being late, and the inconvenience it caused other people. She had flared up and told him she didn't care what other people thought, she had too many things to do, and there wasn't anything she could do about it.

He didn't come back at her. But when he was alone he got down on his knees and seriously asked God for help. The next day his wife came to him and said, "Honey, you have every right to tell me to be on time." When a man in faith and patience has set his heart to obey Christ, he can trust Christ to work a loving submission in his wife.

Likewise a wife, who in faith and patience submits to her husband's authority, moves God to make him a responsible, caring head. There is no more secure position for a wife than living in submission to a husband who himself is in submission to Christ.

This is God's order for marriage, an order He himself establishes, supports and honors wherever He finds the faith to receive it. It is not an ideal we achieve by our own striving. It is an order which we humbly ask God to establish in the marriage He has entrusted to us, a precious gift of the Spirit, received in faith, which builds friendship between husband and wife.

Headship and submission turn on the word *responsibility*. A husband does not dwell on "being the head" nor a wife on "being submissive." That simply describes the way they relate to each other. Each one must ask, "What is my responsibility in this relationship?" That is what makes the relationship work.

Headship Establishes Direction

The primary function of headship is to establish and maintain direction. Headship is responsible to plot the ship's course and bring it to its appointed destination.

Part of the conflict and confusion which we see in homes today stems from a too simplistic exercise of headship. To be head of the house means more than a man occupying the captain's quarters and barking out orders. It means learning to shoulder the responsibility for giving informed and intelligent direction to the family.

A husband won't have all the good ideas. His wife and children, as well as people from outside the immediate family, may have important things to say about what the family ought to be doing. It is the husband's responsibility to weigh every suggestion, determine what should be done,* and see that it happens.

A husband certainly will not make all the decisions in a well-ordered family. Wives are expected to "rule their household" (1 Tim. 5:14). The "good

---

*In the following chapter we will take up the whole question of how decisions are arrived at in a Christian marriage.

wife" portrayed in Proverbs 31 gives direction to a wide range of activities that pertain to the well-being of the household. In any good marriage a lot of direction will depend upon the ideas and decisions of the wife. The important thing for the husband is that this represents sensible delegation, not abdication, on his part.

Setting direction involves setting *priorities*. The kind of things a family gives time and attention to will significantly determine where they end up as a family.

Every morning at seven o'clock I call our household to morning prayers. I believe it is one of the most important things I do all day long. It is the best half-hour of the day, a time when all the family is together, and when we consciously focus our attention on God, and our relationship with Him.

It has not always been this way. The first ten years of our marriage we couldn't seem to get any kind of family worship going. The main reason was that I did not put a high enough priority on it.

Family worship is the symbolic center of a family's spiritual commitment. It says, "This family looks to God for its basic direction."

In setting the direction of the marriage, a Christian husband must give first priority to the family's spiritual nurture and calling. A practicing atheist is more honest than a Christian who has relegated God to a fifth-rate priority for his family. The atheist at least is consistent: He doesn't make any pretense of belief or commitment. The Christian, by definition, claims to be living under the lordship of Christ, yet does not order the life of the family in such a way that His lordship becomes a practical reality. Jesus' life is reality; His invisible presence in our families can become a daily reality. It is His presence that sets the fundamental direction of a Christian marriage.

The second priority which the husband must establish is the family itself. This is not selfish indulgence. It is good management of a precious resource. The family is charged with the enormous responsibility of training the next generation and sustaining the present ones. A husband who keeps the well-being of the family high on his list of responsibilities actually performs the greatest possible service to the larger society. How many ills of society would be cured—indeed, prevented—if families were functioning as they should?

I believe that a Christian couple can build the kind of life together of which, in all humility, they can say, "If the rest of society lived their family life the way that we by God's grace live ours, this would be a far better country to live in."

The third priority which a husband must establish is his vocation. A man whose relationship with God and with his family is in good order is in the best possible position to get direction in regard to his work.

Our technological culture has reversed this order. The job has become a number one priority. Spiritual and human values have suffered at the expense of material acquisitions. God and family have been pushed aside in the drive to succeed and amass possessions.

Jesus said, "What will it profit a man, if he shall gain the whole world, and lose his own soul?" (Matt. 16:26). Our age could add a corollary: "What profit to gain the whole world, and lose your own family?"

A group of men in our congregation get together

for prayer every morning at six o'clock. One of the things we pray for is the *jobs* of our fellow members. During some upheavals in the general economy we have seen remarkable things happen: Positions staying open during widespread layoffs, new jobs opening up, businesses coming through severe crises. God is not unconcerned about our vocations, or our material needs. Indeed, He wants us to trust Him in those areas of our life. For He has promised, "I will never leave you nor forsake you" (Heb. 13:5). But He wants us to establish direction for this part of our life in line with the higher priorities of spiritual and family life.

Headship Exercises Authority

When a man lives under the authority of Christ, Christ is able to entrust him with authority over his family. It is not the husband's authority, as such, which functions in a Christian home, but it is Christ's authority operating through the husband.

Husbands who do not know their standing under Christ tend to veer off in one of two directions, and the cause is the same in both cases: *They lack confidence in their authority.* On the one hand they may exercise authority too timidly, or even abdicate their headship altogether. Or they may go to the opposite extreme and become unreasonable and tyrannical, to compensate for their feeling of inadequacy.

A husband who knows that he is Christ's representative can exercise authority without being either reticent or overbearing. He does not apologize for the word he brings to his wife or children, for it is not his own word, but Christ's. Yet he does it humbly, trusting the Holy Spirit to ratify the word in their hearts.

We are not suggesting that a husband has a magic hotline to heaven. His seeking to understand the specific will of God for his family is fraught with all the ambiguity which ever marks a life lived by faith, not by sight. (How we come to know God's will is taken up in the next chapter.) It is not presumptuous for the husband to speak as God's representative to his family. That is what it means to exercise headship under Christ. What is presumptuous is to order the life of my family in ways of my own choosing, rather than according to the Word of God.

In a family life seminar someone asked Nordis, "How does your husband exercise authority over you?"

"He says 'No' to me," she answered laconically. She went on to explain that is one of the ways a husband protects his wife.

In actual fact I seldom say No to my wife. Most of the time we discuss things and come to agreement. Yet occasionally something comes up where a No is called for. To duck out of that occasion would be as irresponsible as using my authority to lord it over my wife. A husband's headship must be as flexible and sensitive as the headship of Christ, who sometimes woos, sometimes commands, and sometimes allows us to learn by our mistakes.

One of the deepest bonds of friendship between husband and wife is forged by the headship which the husband exercises over the children. Much of a child's early training comes through the mother. This is according to nature; it is true in all cultures. Yet the authority of the father must be a constant presence, supporting her, backing her up.

Because it flows from Christ the authority of a Christian father will manifest the gentleness of

Christ. A husband may see that his wife is distracted and irritable with all the clamor of the children at breakfast time—lunches to fix, breakfast to prepare. Janet dashes in with an "emergency!" She needs a shoebox-theater for second-hour English class, and Todd forgot to bring his history paper home to be signed, so he begs Mom to drive him to school and sign it so he won't get docked ten points.

That night the father sits down with his family and lays out a plan. Susan (the teen-ager) will make up the lunches for everyone the night before. No more "emergency" demands will be permitted in the morning. Each child will take time in the evening to go over his plans for the next day and see that everything is taken care of. Mother and Dad will get up a half hour earlier in the morning to have a quiet time of Bible reading and prayer, letting the peace of Christ take command of their thoughts and plans. And the entire family will gather for prayer before breakfast.

The father brings the focus of the family to rest upon Christ, the source of their harmony and peace. He uses his authority not to lord it over his wife and children, but gently to build them up, teach them, encourage them, plan for them, and direct them.

Yet his authority is not without the firmness, even the sternness, of Christ either. Where the do-it-yourself father might become lax or uncertain of himself, the father living under Christ is firm and unyielding. It is never a question in his household what the family will do Sunday morning. They are together in church, worshiping God. The father permits no breach of honesty or clean speech in his home. The obedience of the children is not a "sometime" thing. It is a settled issue, because Christ expects it.

The atmosphere in our home changed overnight when my wife and I came to see that discipline (spanking, when necessary) was not our thing but God's. A spanking is not a father inflicting his will on the child. It is the father's obedient response to God's Word, upon encountering rebellion or disobedience in a child. When we saw this, spankings became harder, more consistent—and far less frequent!

Discipline carried out in obedience to a moral law which is applicable to both father and child has a different spiritual and emotional tone to it than discipline which is merely an expression of the father's personal will. And the child is quick to sense the difference. He is more responsive to the discipline because it is operating through God's chain-of-command. A father who knows his standing under Christ will not hesitate to exercise firm discipline where it is needed in order that Christ's will for the family come to practical realization.

Headship Builds Up

Headship and submission are the superstructure upon which marriage is built. The strength and stability of the marriage depend upon this relationship being maintained. If a wife loses her submission to her husband, she loses her unity with him. If a husband abdicates his responsibility as head, he strikes at the very core of the relationship which God has established between him and his wife.

The relationship is designed to build up both husband and wife, according to the divine model. The Father exalts the Son. He delights to lift Him up, to honor Him. This is the way headship behaves when it is grounded in love. The courtesy which a husband shows toward his wife, the way he honors her before the children, his open and evident esteem for her, is the foundation upon which the wife's respect and trust in her husband is built. And then she, in turn, will acknowledge and exalt her husband, gladly submitting to his authority—as Jesus exalts the Father and submits to His authority.

Wives today are not subjugated and oppressed, in need of "liberation." How anyone could grow up in our culture during the past forty years and arrive at such a notion is incomprehensible. It is precisely the *absence* of male authority which plagues American families.

Husbands and fathers have abdicated their responsibility. We are fast becoming a matriarchal society. The teaching and discipline of the children, responsibility for the upkeep and management of the home, the family image in the community, participation in church and civic affairs and, increasingly, major responsibility for the financial support of the family—all of this has been laid on the woman's shoulders.

Small wonder that she begins to voice some complaint. But we live in an age when values and understanding have become so twisted out of shape that the remedy being offered is more of the same! More opportunities for women to take on the responsibilities of men—like a runner panting to the finish line of a mile run, and being told to elbow into the starting line for a two-mile run.

Yet despite the anti-housewife, anti-motherhood, anti-marriage propaganda that is abroad today, most women will still end up getting married and having children. No amount of tinkering with employment practices, career counseling, or "consciousness raising" will get at the root of the problem faced by the great majority of women.

The problem is mass abdication on the part of husbands. The need in American families today is not some kind of manufactured "equality" between husband and wife. The equality is already there— God-given, waiting to be discovered. The need is for *headship*. Let men accept the responsibility of being head of the family, and wives will find under their authority a freedom, a liberation, such as no constitutional amendment could ever guarantee.

A Christian man does not lord it over his family, as head of the house. As we have pointed out, he uses that position as a base from which to serve his wife and children. This does not mean he becomes their servant, in the sense that he moves this way and that at their bidding, trying to please them and satisfy all their desires. The father serves them *by accepting the responsibility of being head of the house.*

He serves them by working well at his trade or profession, in order to provide for their material needs. He serves them by taking time to give them the kind of leadership and direction which will knit them together and build them up as a family and as individuals. He serves them by earnestly becoming more and more disciplined to Christ. He serves them by encouraging their intellectual and artistic potential. He serves them by taking command and, with them, setting realistic goals which concur with God's Word and God's will. In a word, he serves his family by *providing* for them—physically, emotionally, socially, intellectually, culturally, and spiritually. This is the kind of love Jesus taught us to expect from God, the model of all fatherhood. He gives us daily bread ... He protects us from evil ... He brings us into the Kingdom.

TO
WHOM
AM I
RESPONSIBLE?

CHAPTER THIRTEEN

The Last Word

True or False: In family decision-making, the husband has the last word.

Answer: False.

In Chapter Eleven Nordis said that practically speaking, submission means that if husband and wife do not agree, the husband has the responsibility for making the final decision. Well, isn't that the same as saying that he has the last word?

As head the husband is responsible to Christ for what happens in his family. He is responsible to discover and implement Christ's will, not decree his own will for the family. His responsibility may require him to *speak* the last word. But it is Christ who *has* the last word, if the family is living according to God's order.

How can a husband and wife discover what God's will for them is? We are thinking beyond general categories, such as keeping the Commandments, praying, showing love and kindness toward others, and worship of God. Knowing these general truths, can a family discover *specific ways* that God would want any of these truths implemented? Can they, further, know His will in regard to some of the practical decisions of everyday life? Things like

    celebrating birthdays
    buying a new car
    firing an employee

    making up with a friend
    joining a church
    choosing a college
    considering a new job
    taking in an elderly relative
    going on a diet
    supporting a political candidate
    taking a vacation
    serving as a hospital volunteer
    planning a budget
    disciplining a teenager
    witnessing to a fellow worker
    choosing friends
    writing off a bad debt

The Bible says, "If any of you lacks wisdom, let him ask of God, who gives to all men generously and without reproaching, and it will be given him" (James 1:5). It goes on to say that we must "ask in faith." We must expect God to give us the wisdom we ask for.

One of the distinguishing marks of the early Christians was that *they experienced guidance.* They sought and received the wisdom of God for a variety of situations—handling lying and cheating in the fellowship, starting missionary work, responding to a heckler, resolving an argument, planning journeys, dealing with emergencies (Acts 5:3, 13:3, 13:8, 15:28, 16:6, 19:21, 27:23).

God reveals His will not only in broad general terms. If we are willing to seek His guidance, He will make known His will in regard to the everyday decisions that affect the life and well-being of our families. There is no greater security than to be embarked on a course of action which you know to be God's will. Even in the midst of upheaval or conflict you can experience His peace because you know that He will not desert you. One of the privileges and responsibilities of a husband is to lead his wife and children into the security of God's will.

How, in practical terms, does the husband do this? And what part do the wife and children play in the process?

Two things are involved: The *conditions* for receiving guidance, and the *way* of receiving guidance.

The Conditions for Receiving Guidance

The first condition for receiving guidance is *recognizing God's order for the family.* Headship is a means God has appointed for channeling the lordship of Christ into our homes. If we honor it, He will work through it.

This means that from the outset everyone knows that the weight of final decision rests with the husband and father. He is the one charged with the responsibility of seeing that God's will is known and carried out in the family.

When God's order of headship is recognized at the very outset it creates the most favorable climate for receiving guidance. It gives the family a way of relating together so they can act in unity. Instead of competing with one another, each one striving for his own way, they work as a team to find God's way. They are like the crew of an airplane coming in for a difficult landing. The crew members do everything they can to assist the head pilot, so he can bring them in. The pilot knows that a successful landing depends upon the input and help he receives from the co-pilot, navigator, and other crew members.

One time when we were on a trip we asked our children what they considered important for good family life. Arne, our youngest, piped up from the back seat, "The kids should get listened to, but they shouldn't be pushy." That's a fair description of how headship ought to function. I need to listen to my wife and children. They need to trust me to receive and act wisely upon what they have said.

A second condition for receiving guidance is *the surrender of our own wills*. "Not my will, but *thy* will be done" (Luke 22:42). Jesus sweat drops of blood praying that prayer. It's not easy to give up our own wills. But until we do, we are not truly open to receive God's will.

The husband, especially, needs to keep this continually in view. Because he has the authority to speak the last word, he can drift into the habit of stating a decision without having seriously sought God's will in the matter. I find that periodically God allows a situation to come up that challenges a preference or opinion of mine. The situation may be irritatingly slight in itself—like Nordis wanting to have in some friends on an evening when I'd rather watch TV. But God wants to see whether I have become sluggish in my exercise of headship. Whether I have forgotten that, even in little things, *He* has the last word. For He knows that if my will begins to take over in the family, we will miss the blessing and protection of His will.

In 1971 I was invited to spend a sabbatical year at the Institute for Ecumenical and Cultural Research on the campus of St. John's University in Collegeville, Minnesota. Nordis and I thought it would be a good chance for some quiet study and extra family time after ten years as pastor of a very active congregation. The younger children, too, thought it would be fun to go back to Minnesota for a year where they would be "out in the country," and close to their grandparents.

However, Tim, our oldest son, was going into his senior year in high school. He didn't relish the idea of a new school and new friends for his last year in high school. We knew that this would be a special year for our family and we wanted Tim to be a part of it. But he wanted to stay in San Pedro and graduate with the friends he'd gone all through school with. The matter dragged on for several months and occasioned some unpleasant wrangling around the house.

One afternoon Tim was down at the church and I asked him to come in to my office.

"Let's talk about Minnesota," I said.

"Okay," he said without much enthusiasm.

"Something came to me this morning. We've both been telling each other what *we* want, but the real question is what God wants. What came to me was this, that if God doesn't want you to go back to Minnesota, then neither do I."

He brightened a little.

"Would you say the same thing, that if God didn't want you to stay in San Pedro, you wouldn't want to stay?"

He thought a few moments and said, "I guess so."

"Tim, here's the way I see it. If we insist that you go, and you insist on staying here, we will not be open to hearing what God wants. I think both of us have to set aside our own wills. Your mother and I have to say, 'We're ready to make arrangements so Tim can stay in San Pedro.' And you have to say, 'I'm ready to go to Minnesota.' If we'll both do that, I believe God will let us know what *He* has to say."

He saw that, for the first time, I was seriously considering giving up what I had been insisting on. He weighed the meaning of it, for it required the same thing of him. After a few moments he nodded and said, "Okay."

So we prayed about it together, and went home for supper more at peace with one another than we had been for several months.

God worked it out in an interesting way. Several days later Nordis came up with the idea, "Look, Tim could go back to Minnesota with us for the first semester. That way he would share the experience with the rest of us. Then we could send him back to San Pedro for the second semester so he could graduate with his friends."

We talked and prayed about it. The idea seemed right and took root. Tim began to talk about what he would do back in Minnesota, while we discussed arrangements for him to return to San Pedro.

As it turned out he enjoyed Minnesota more than he had expected and decided to stay out the year there. During the second semester he decided that he wanted to attend a college in Minnesota the next fall. He stayed right on through the summer and didn't get back home to San Pedro for eighteen months!

God had more in view than any of us had realized. Minnesota figured significantly in His plan for Tim's life. But He also saw our need, as parents, to begin to get adjusted to the idea that our children were growing up and entering a more independent phase of life. We can look back now and see the beauty of His plan. I do not believe we would have experienced it in the way we did if Tim and I had not talked together that afternoon and agreed to lay down our wills.

The Way of Receiving Guidance

The idea of "guidance" spooks some people. They think of people falling into trances or hearing voices. They know the Bible talks about God "speaking to people" but that was back then. Or maybe it was meant only in a figurative sense. Today we have, well, the Bible and common sense.

Others feel that it is presumptuous. Once, while giving a talk on prayer, I stressed the importance of praying according to the will of God. "If you don't know it's God's will, don't pray for it," I said.

A woman objected, "How can we presume to know God's will?"

Yet both by precept and example the Bible teaches that Christians should know God's will. "Do not be conformed to this world but be transformed by the renewal of your mind, *that you may prove what is the will of God,* what is good and acceptable and perfect" (Rom. 12:2). When there was disagreement in the early church, the leaders gathered together in Jerusalem, discussed and prayed together, and came to agreement about God's will in the matter (Acts 15).

Discerning God's will is not something that happens only in the Bible, or in lofty circles of the spiritually elite. It should be the experience of ordinary Christians. It may come in extraordinary ways, but God also lets us discover His will through the ordinary avenues of reason and common sense.

One cannot be flippant about knowing God's

will. It is not a casual thing. It is something we should seek to grow in our whole life long. To walk perfectly in the will of God is the culmination of a lifetime, yet we can begin today.

*   *   *

God speaks to us in a twofold way—*outwardly* and *inwardly*. He secretes His thought in outward things that we encounter in our everyday life. The outward thing by itself does not tell us much. It is, as it were, only the raw material for guidance. It requires the inward working of the Holy Spirit to give shape to the meaning that God has hidden in the outward thing.

At Philippi the Apostle Paul went to the riverside outside the city and struck up a conversation with some women who were washing clothes. His words were an "outward thing." On some, apparently, the words had little or no effect. But one woman, Lydia, saw something more in Paul's words. "The Lord opened her heart to give heed to what was said by Paul" (Acts 16:14). Which is another way of saying that the Holy Spirit showed her the meaning that God had put in Paul's words.

For guidance we depend upon both of these factors—the outward thing which God has invested with meaning, and the inward grasp of that meaning which is given by the Holy Spirit. But our approach to each is somewhat different. The outward things we approach actively with a view to gathering the raw material of information and experience—

We study the *Bible.*
We *worship, learn* and *serve* in church.
We evaluate *circumstances.*
We listen carefully to the *counsel of others.*
We are related to others in the *Christian fellowship.*

The inward conviction comes as we quietly rely upon the enlightenment of the Holy Spirit—

We seek unity with God in *prayer.*
We seek unity with others in *consensus.*
We seek unity within ourselves in *the witness of the Holy Spirit.*

God speaks to us in this twofold way because He must overcome two barriers in order to bring His truth home to our hearts. First, the outward things overcome the barrier of our *ignorance.* There are things we do not know, or need to be reminded of. Apart from the objective meaning that God stores up in the outward things we would not have the wherewithal to know His will. The important thing here is to *take it in.*

In 1962 my parents came out from Minnesota to spend Christmas with us. My father is a soft-spoken man and only rarely had he ever said anything to me by way of advice after I was married. But one Sunday he took me aside and said, "Larry, can't you do anything about your children? They were running wild on the church patio between services. It's too much for Nordis."

A little later the word drifted back to me that the wife of one of our leading laymen had said, "I think we can get used to the Pastor and Nordis, but *those kids* . . !"

God had something to say to us so He sent some words to my ears—ordinary, objective words. But words which expressed His will in regard to the way we were raising our children. Those words helped lead us into a serious study of family life.

Secondly, the inward working of the Holy Spirit overcomes the barrier of our *pride* and *self-will.* There is within us a natural resistance to God's will.

"The carnal (i.e., natural human) attitude is inevitably opposed to the purpose of God" (Rom. 8:7, Phillips). The Holy Spirit makes clear to us the truth that God is bringing to us through some outward thing so we will cease resisting, and say Yes to His will. The important thing here is to *give up our pride and self-will.*

Bud and Jean Hahn wanted to move from San Pedro back to San Diego. They didn't like Bud's job, and they missed the friends and surroundings of their former home. Bud found a job in San Diego and began to commute, coming home on weekends while they waited for the house to sell. But, as Bud said later, "we couldn't *give* that house away. Nobody even came to look at it."

One day a man came by with an offer for Bud to go into business with him. They had discussed the possibility some time earlier but had not been able to come to terms. The man was ready to make a new proposal.

Bud and Jean began to look at the circumstances that were taking shape around them. Was God saying something? They had their hearts set on moving to San Diego but events seemed to be conspiring to keep them in San Pedro. The more they thought about it the more clear it seemed that God wanted them to give up the move to San Diego. They finally decided to accept the business offer, take the house off the market, and stay in San Pedro.

"As I look back on it," Bud says, "it scares me to think how close we came to moving away from the place where God had a special plan for us." He eventually became the principal owner of the business, and both he and his wife became trusted leaders when a spiritual awakening came to our congregation. It all hinged on giving up their plans to move to San Diego.

When we understand this twofold way in which God speaks to us—through outward things and inward conviction—we will be more balanced in our whole approach to guidance. First of all we will make certain that we have sufficient input from outside. Foremost among the outward things, the primary storehouse of God's truth, is the Scripture. He has stored up inexhaustible reserves of meaning for our lives in the words of the Bible. In order to receive guidance a Christian couple needs to be well grounded in the written Word of God.

Another outward thing is the church, the fellowship of believers. Our family needs to be related in a brotherly way to a Christian community which is also seeking God's will, where others more mature than we are can teach, encourage, admonish, and correct us.

Another outward means God uses to channel His truth into a marriage, which we especially want to focus upon, is the words husband and wife speak to each other. A man who feels keenly the responsibility of headship will not only listen to his wife, he will actively seek her counsel. A wife is one of God's most vital channels for conveying His wisdom to the husband (and vice-versa). To see this dimension in our conversation deepens our love and regard for one another. If God so honors us, should we not honor one another?

And we do not have in view exalted spiritual discourses between husband and wife. God lets His truth ride in on our everyday conversation. A wife may thoroughly disagree with a plan her husband comes up with. Her objections, fears, insights, evaluation—

even her tears and pleading—can be vehicles for God's truth which the husband must take in and consider.

It is no breach of a wife's submission to speak her mind freely when she disagrees with her husband. Indeed, if she conceals what she knows or feels, for fear of displeasing him, she fails in her duty to him.

Wives must submit to their husbands in two ways, "transitively" and "intransitively." The Bible tells wives to submit to their husbands. "Submit" in this case is what grammarians call an "intransitive verb." It means that a wife yields or defers to her husband's authority. But "submit" is also used as a transitive verb where it means to present something for someone else's use or discretion, as when you "submit a report." A wife must submit to her husband both "transitively" and "intransitively"—and in that order! She must submit a full report of the way she thinks and feels about things that affect their marriage. The husband needs her wisdom and insight in order to exercise responsible headship. Having done this she can confidently submit to his authority, trusting the Holy Spirit to give him right judgment.

When husband and wife relate to each other in this way, both actively seeking the will of God, they can expect to arrive at most of their decisions by consensus. To be in agreement with his wife is an encouraging assurance for the husband, who must bear final responsibility for decisions that are made. Bringing husband and wife to unity on an issue is one of the ways the Spirit confirms to them that they are in tune with the will of God. "If two of you agree on earth about anything they ask, it will be done for them by my Father in heaven" (Matt. 18:19).

If they do not agree, and a decision cannot be postponed, then the husband must decide what they will do. He may decide, even though he does not agree with his wife, that her opinion should prevail. He may feel that her insights and feelings are closer to the issue than his, or he may simply have the inner sense that she has the mind of God more than he does on this particular issue. That kind of yielding is a proper exercise of headship, whereas yielding because he is afraid of displeasing his wife is an abdication of headship. On the other hand, he may decide in favor of his own view. In either case the decision is his. If he follows the wife's wishes, and it turns out badly, he cannot come back and throw the blame on her. The responsibility is his. That is what it means to be a head.

No wife is going to give flawless advice. No husband is going to make perfect decisions every time. For which there is one all-encompassing answer, "Forgive one another daily from the heart." *

On that note we would end. For it is the surest place for a Christian couple to begin.

---

* Bonhoeffer, Dietrich. "A Wedding Sermon From a Cell" in *Letters From Prison*, SCM Press Ltd., London, 1967.

CHRIST HAS THE LAST WORD

EPILOG

Saints

Greet all the saints. —Hebrews 13:24

CHAPTER FOURTEEN

Get Up and Go On

"You shall say to them, Thus says the Lord: When men fall, do they not rise again?"—Jeremiah 8:4

These words are directed to the Old Testament saints, the people of God.

The word 'saint' has come to have a dual meaning. In the New Testament a saint is simply a Christian, somebody who has accepted Christ as Lord and Savior and is living out the Christian life. But in popular usage the word has come to mean a Christian who has lived a life as close to perfection as a human being could live.

I have a collection of short biographies of most of the men and women who have come to be acknowledged as saints. If you were to plow through that volume you'd find that it involves a great deal of variety—the kind of backgrounds these people came from, the kind of lives they lived, the kind of things that they did. And yet there's one thread that goes through all of them: *They never gave up.* They may have struggled and stumbled and fallen down many a time, but they didn't lie down and quit. They got up and went on.

If there is one sure way of becoming a saint, it's just this business of staying with it, not quitting. Struggle and stumbling and falling there will be, but *get up and go on.*

Have you gone through struggles in your Christian experience? Even this week have you stumbled and fallen? Get up, take a fresh start at this business of living the Christian life! No person yet has lived the Christian life on a straight line upward toward the Kingdom of Heaven. All have made mistakes (see James 3:2). We stumble and fall, and when we do we must get up and go on.

This involves three basic things:

1. I must agree with God that I have fallen.
2. I must deal with the cause of my falling.
3. I must actively return to the way of the Lord.

I Must Agree That I Have Fallen

I must confess my mistakes, my sin, my error. One man has said, "Most Americans see no real reason to return to God. They never thought they left." The Israelites thought that way too. They said that the law of the Lord was with them. But the Lord said that the scribes had distorted it (Jer. 8:8).

There are scribes, teachers of the Word of God, who are doing that same thing today. There's a distorting of the mind of God, a relaxing of the commandments of God, teaching men that they can have the Christian faith any way they want it.

We sat once in a seminar where a theological professor blatantly denied the Virgin Birth, and was not called to task by those in authority. He said, "If you want to get all involved in this biological business of the virgin birth, I suppose it's all right..." But he made it clear that he looked on that as a kind of child's play. The "real significance" was a lofty spiritual and philosophical principle. One pastor had the presence of mind to stand up and say, "The point the Bible makes is precisely the biological fact of the virgin birth.''

A man begins a lecture on pastoral counseling by saying, ''Now if you believe in free love, as I do. . .'' A brochure for a ministers' seminar carries the title, ''The Creative Alternative of Divorce.'' A far cry from the words of Malachi, where the Lord says, ''I hate divorce.''

What about our own personal lives? There, also, we have to face reality and agree with God that we have fallen. Consider just a first step in our personal relationship with God, our time of prayer. If our times of corporate worship do not grow out of the soil of daily private prayer, it can too easily be a window dressing. It may make a good impression, but it lacks reality because it does not grow out of the soil of a personal communion with God.

Or the study of Scripture. Do we know what He has told us? Do we know the kind of life He has outlined for us? Have we been content to ''know'' at an intellectual level, but have stumbled when it comes to living it out?

What about our own personal disciplines—the way we eat, the time we go to bed, the way we order our family life, the way we play, the way we manage our finances? Or our concern for the community in which we live? All the things that either add or detract from our witness as Christians?

Have I stumbled and fallen? If so, then I have to agree with God that I have fallen. That's the first step, agreeing with *God* when we have fallen.

I Must Deal with the Cause of My Falling

What have I done?

The Lord says, ''No one asks, 'What have I done?' '' (Jer. 8:6). We must intelligently consider why we have missed the mark, why we have fallen. Otherwise we may wind up doing the same thing again.

David fell into sin with Bathsheba because he was idle at home instead of being out with his troops where he should have been. Idleness led to the sin of lust, lust led to adultery, adultery led to murder. One sin leads to another.

A boy and girl go to a party, and the party gets out of hand, with drinking and rowdy behavior. When the party is over they have the inner feeling that they've become stained and polluted. They have to consider intelligently, "Why?" Along the line, when they saw that that party was getting out of hand, they didn't separate themselves, even at the cost of some embarrassment.

Why did you blow up at that neighbor next door who always irks you? Why didn't you control your tongue? You begin to look at it seriously, and ask yourself, "Have I really prayed for that person?" The Bible tells us to pray for those who despitefully use us.

Why have I gone back on a vow? What about the way I ignore my wife's questions? What about the way I speak to my children when I must correct them? What about the way I spend money, without my husband's agreement?

I slip and fall. *What* have I done? What is the cause of my falling? That's the first question to be answered. It brings you to the point of understanding. The second is this: What have I *done?* This brings you to the point of repentance and forgiveness, "Lord, what have I *done!*"

I might be able to convince my conscious mind it was all right. That's called rationalization. I might get my friends to agree with me: "You couldn't have done otherwise. You were driven to it." But the Spirit of Jesus that lives within us will not accept a lie, will not accept a rationalization. The Spirit of Jesus demands the truth and lives the truth.

Our very bodies may suffer in order to make us face up to the truth. People come up with all manner of sickness and disease because they try to foist a lie, an unconfessed sin, upon their spirit.

A chaplain once counseled with a woman, and on a sudden inspiration asked her, "Have you ever had an abortion?" She said, "Yes, I haven't thought of it for years. But that has nothing to do with my problem." He said, "You may think that has nothing to do with your problem, but ever since that happened every cell of your body has been crying out, 'Murderer! Murderer! Murderer!' Until you deal with that, you'll have no peace from the thing that's bothering you."

The Spirit demands absolute honesty. In Psalm 32 David says, "When I declared not my sin, my body wasted away through my groaning all day long, for day and night thy hand was heavy upon me; my strength was dried up as by the heat of summer." He experienced no relief until he confessed his sin.

Having confessed, one must take the next step, must seek and accept the forgiveness of Christ. This can be harder than admitting the sin. It is harder for some people to believe that God will forgive them than to face up to the sin itself.

Christ wants to identify himself with us in the place of our falling. Maybe other people won't. Maybe other people will condemn us. But Christ forgives us. It's as though He puts His arm around us and takes us to himself: "This one now belongs to me. If you have any claim against this one, you have to take it up with me."

We may have to suffer the consequences of our sin in this life, but not alone, for Christ is standing with us because of that forgiveness. David's sin brought down upon him some terrible consequences. The prophet Nathan said, "Evil is going to arise up out of your own house. The sword is never going to depart from your house. Your own children are going to cause you grief." All this came to pass. Yet God never deserted David. When David said, "I have sinned against the Lord," the word came immediately from Nathan, the prophet, "The Lord has also forgiven your sin." The consequences he still had to endure. But he was ever known as the friend of God. He was ever known as the one in whom the Lord delighted, a man after God's own heart. Because he was perfect? No, because he got up and went on. Because he didn't stay there. He accepted the forgiveness of God and moved on.

That's the way you obtain anything in the kingdom, you get up and go on. God does not look for perfect performance, He looks for sustained performance.

I Must Actively Return to the Way of the Lord

By instinct, if a man falls, he gets up. In natural human experience, if he goes off course, he veers back on course. If I'm driving down the highway, and I wander over the middle line, I very quickly correct and pull back to avoid a head-on collision.

But, strangely, in spiritual life we can veer off and go careening down the wrong side of the road heading for a spiritual head-on collision and seem to take no note of it. "My people do not know my ordinances. Even the birds of the heaven know when to correct themselves, when to turn and migrate in a different direction. It's built into their nature. But my people are dull of understanding. They don't understand that in spiritual things there is a principle of correction: You admit before God that you've fallen, then you get up and go on." (See Jeremiah 8:7.)

A friend once told me of a time when he came into great despair. He still had to preach to other people about the victorious life in Christ, but he himself felt utterly empty. His wife had died and he felt drained. Yet he kept moving ahead. He got up every day and went on, even though his feelings cried out against it. He wouldn't lie down and quit. And gradually God brought him through it.

During that time he wasn't able to do many of the things he normally did. He wasn't able to counsel with his usual confidence. He'd turn people away and get off by himself. He "stumbled and fell." But he got up and went on, and because he did his life continued to grow in Christ.

God does not expect of us a perfect, flawless performance, starting from the moment we're converted until we stroll through the gates of heaven with straight A's. Such a person never existed. Read through the lives of the saints and you'll see fall, after fall, after fall. But the one thing that differentiates the saint from the backslider is that the saint gets up and goes on. And he goes on in greater strength because he's learned something from his mistakes.

If we get up and go on, our mistakes become blessings. If we just stay there and wallow in them, they become the thing that defeats us.

Saints are not people peculiarly endowed with all kinds of heavenly characteristics, so that they're almost another species. They are very ordinary people. They stumble and fall. But they don't quit.

That's all that God asks of us, that we get up and go on. His forgiveness is big enough to take care of our mistakes, our fallings and failings. But nothing in heaven or earth can cause us to move on with God if we lie down and quit.

If you've been frustrated or upset or disappointed with your own Christian experience, don't feel that you're out in a far corner of the ballpark, while the real game is being played somewhere else. You're right in the middle of things. You're where saints are made, the place of stumbling and falling.

Agree with God that you've fallen, deal realistically with the cause of your falling, and through His forgiving grace move actively back into the way of the Lord.

Get up and go on!

Because Christ Forgives, Because He Gives Grace, GET UP AND GO ON!

Notes

Notes to Chapter Two

1. "Is the American Family in Danger?" *U.S. News and World Report,* April 6, 1973, p. 71.

2. *Ibid.*

3. "The American Family," *U.S. News and World Report*, October 27, 1975, p. 32.

4. *Op. cit.*, p. 35.

5. Aries, Phillipe (trans. Robert Baldick). *Centuries of Childhood: A Social History of Family Life.* New York, 1962; originally published as *L'Enfant et la vie Familiale sous l'Anden Regime,* Paris, 1960.

6. Haraven, Tamara K. "The History of the Family as an Interdisciplinary Field," *The Journal of Interdisciplinary History,* Vol. 2, 1971, p. 211.

7. Walters, Ronald G. "The Family and Ante-bellum Reform: An Interpretation." *Societas—A Review of Social History,* v. 3, summer, 1973, pp. 222-223.

8. "Hartford Affirmation." *Christianity Today,* February 14, 1975, p. 53.

9. A philosophical analysis which admirably demonstrates the incompatibility of biblical Christianity with secular humanism (and which also shows the inroads that humanism, materialism, and naturalism have made in major schools of theology) is to be found in Morton Kelsey's *Encounter With God,* especially chapters 2-5. Bethany Fellowship, Inc., Minneapolis, 1972.

Notes to Chapter Eight

1. Trobisch, Ingrid. *The Joy of Being a Woman,* Harper & Row, New York, 1975, p. 61.

2. Kippley, John and Sheila, *The Art of Natural Family Planning.* Couple-to-Couple League, Inc., Cincinnati, Ohio, 1975, p. 6.

3. Kippley, *op. cit.*, p. 3.

4. Elisabeth Kübler-Ross, "An Interview," *People,* November 24, 1975.

5. Kippley, *op. cit.*, p. 155.

6. Hilgers, Thos. W., M.D. "The Intrauterine Device: Contraceptive or Abortifacient?" *Marriage and Family Newsletter,* Vol. 5, Jan. 1974.

7. Lorincz, Albert, M.D. "The Pill—How Does It Work?" Lecture at Marriage and Family Life Workshop, St. John's University, Collegeville, Minnesota, June 8, 1972.

8. Kippley, *op. cit.*, p. xvi.

9. Kippley, *op. cit.*, p. 4.

Notes to Chapter Eleven

1. Trobisch, Ingrid. *The Joy of Being a Woman,* Harper & Row, New York, 1975, p. 7.

2. Selye, Dr. Hans. "Secret of Coping with Stress." *U.S. News and World Report,* March 21, 1977, p. 51.

3. Schaeffer, Edith. *What Is a Family?* Fleming H. Revell Company, Old Tappan, N.J., 1975, p. 48.

4. *Ibid.*

Recommended Reading

Chapter Seven

The Act of Marriage by Tim and Beverly LaHaye. Zondervan Publishing House, Grand Rapids, Michigan, 1976. 291 pages.

The Freedom of Sexual Love by Joseph and Lois Bird. Doubleday, New York, 1970. Paperback, 148 pages.

Chapter Eight

The Art of Natural Family Planning by John and Sheila Kippley. The Couple-to-Couple League International, Inc., Box 11084, Cincinnati, Ohio 45211, 1975. 218 pages.

The Joy of Being a Woman by Ingrid Trobisch. Harper & Row, Publishers, New York, 1975. 134 pages.

Natural Family Planning, the Ovulation Method by John Billings, M.D. The Liturgical Press, Collegeville, Minnesota, Second American Edition, 1973. 38 pages.

The Christian Couple Study Guide by Larry Christenson. Bethany Fellowship, Inc., 1979, 48 pages.